T0079881

Collected Poems

EMYR HUMPHREYS

UNIVERSITY OF WALES PRESS
CARDIFF
1999

© Emyr Humphreys, 1999

British Library Cataloguing-in-Publication Data.
A catalogue record for this book is available from the British Library.

ISBN 0–7083–1511–9

All rights reserved. No part of this book may be reproduced, stored in a retrieval system, or transmitted, in any form or by any means, electronic, mechanical, photocopying, recording or otherwise, without clearance from the University of Wales Press, 6 Gwennyth Street, Cardiff, CF2 4YD.

The right of Emyr Humphreys to be identified as author of this work has been asserted by him in accordance with the Copyright, Designs and Patents Act 1988.

Published with the financial support of the Arts Council of Wales

Typeset at University of Wales Press
Printed in Great Britain by Dinefwr Press, Llandybïe

Contents

Author's Note

These pieces are collected in the sense that I have chosen them and in doing so taken the opportunity to make minor revisions, particularly among the earlier poems. By setting them out in approximate chronological order the result comes as close as I would ever venture to that most intractable of literary forms, the autobiography. Whatever the form may be, all writing is part of a continuing effort to ease the intensity of consciousness by extending it.

Gellid honni bod ysgrifennwr yn mwynhau mwy o gyfle dewis ffordd o fyw, a hyd yn oed ei fyd, na'r rhelyw. Ac eto, os yw'n Gymro yn yr oes ddwyieithog hon, hawdd y gall y dewis droi'n dynged neu felltith: pa iaith, pa hunaniaeth, pa wrogaeth?

Yr wyf yn ddyledus i'r Athro M. Wynn Thomas am ei gymorth gyda'r didoli; ac yn cyflwyno'r casgliad i Elinor fy ngwraig.

E.H.

A Young Man Considers his Possibilities

i

I could gather what I can while I may
Attempt for good posts, send excellent references away,
Get to know the people who count,
Establish valuable contacts, then mount,
Begin my 'climb'; accept the current creeds,
Never be awkward in my beliefs, a path that leads
To fines imprisonments and social outlawry.
When at the top I shall remain in bloom
Until someday my family assemble in my room
To watch me die, an honourable old man
Who lived and died according to his plan.

ii

I could devote myself to art
To counting the beating of my heart,
Hold a small mirror to my eye
And thus encompass the whole sky;
Produce my Stephen Dedalus
Complete, living to take a census
Of my living, and then perhaps
Produce *Ulysses* and other maps;
And have these rolled within my tomb
Before the new barbarians come.

iii

I could be Boswell to the dying Wales,
Devote my time to taking minute notes
Of movement; life; and noting where it fails;
Remark careers and graph the tongue's decay,
Industries dying; people going away;
And standing on a rock above the tide
Watch hostile waters rise on every side.

Cymru 1938

I love her marshlands and her mountains
Her stout walls, her woods, her comely domain
Her fallowlands, her valleys and her fountains,
Her white sea-gulls and gracious women.

Yeah. I love the crowds that cram in the movies
The cigarette-smoke in the dim auditorium
The whispers the thrills the wet hand-holdings
My training time with the territorials
November the eleventh before Memorials
The summer-camp outside the town.
I love to swing to Nat Gonella
In the hot dance halls to drink my sasparilla
Through thin straws.

I love the fresh news in the daily-paper,
The half-inch headlines, cartoons and pictures:
(My grandpa's photo appeared last month
'Mr. John Jones of Hendre Uchaf, retired
After fifty years at the factory,
Sight and hearing unimpaired,
His picture shown here with home-made harp').

I love the shady lanes out of town –
A twopenny bus-ride from the station –
Where I walk on summer evenings with my arm
About the waist of a ready girl.

I love her chapel clubs and school societies,
The sweated swotting of matriculation classes,
The general indefatigable desire to get on
The jam at the top and the unemployed teachers
The dwindling congregations and surplus preachers
The younger son who slips into business
i.e. the less gifted and less intelligent,
Who nevertheless does so much better.

I love her milk-ridden paying-guest farms
Her emaciated cattle lying in ferns
Her penniless farmers and underpaid farm-hands
Her tree-tall hedges and Stapleton's agrostic
The bankrupt deacon who turned agnostic
The plough on the hedge and toothless harrow.

I love the councils of our University
Designed to perpetuate servile inferiority
Dowagers to dominate deferential professors
Magnates, ecclesiastics, retired legislators
All ready to subdue or sack unruly educators.

I love the vacant streets in the valleys
Where thin dogs lurch with a coughing man
The beer at the bar for an empty stomach
The chip-fed children sleeping four in a bed,
Father repeating what the Agent should have said.
Mother, at her wits' end. Depression overhead.

I love her seaside watering places
Where fat people swim with vacant faces
The policeman in blue, the wobbling women
Who left their looms for a week and a day
And beyond, beyond the body-littered sand
The advancing storm not far away.

Unloading Hay

Unloading hay, a tumbling heavy summer task,
Thrusting the pitchfork down in the dried-up piled-up ungreened
grass
This inexperienced and soft hand of mine will harden
So I hope, in lifting each loose load with each tight grasp
I take upon this polished pole. This hay is not
So light and cloudy as perhaps it looks from the hill.
Its content is both rough and hard. Dead thistles
That preserve their bite, hard hay, hoar bits of hedges even.
Heaven can be no soft and easy place, but surely
Full of the country air, hard work, and other country customs.
And is not the quivering town all nerves no muscle,
Rush, fear, and never ending fuss a tiny counterpart of Hell?

A Nonconformist

I was not meant to kneel at the cool High Altar
My palate is too coarse for Holy Bread
Vestments for me are cloaks against the Almighty
The arresting song of boys is merely song:
Rather made to pick up an old magazine
One evening when it was too early for bed
And casually read an article of faith
Which for a moment completed my faint picture
Of Jesus quietly pointing at my courage:
'Follow me in the face of hostile crowds
Weapons derision hatred scorn, follow me
From Gethsemane, from sweat to blood to the horrible Cross
To look down at the will of God
In a drunken jostling swearing filthy mob.'

Courage

Who of the indifferent future will read
Of the dead when they were prepossessed with death
Will judge by what they did not what they said
The hour the minute the moment the last breath.

Therefore prepare the stage for a decent action
Present the right alignment for a crime
International crisis is a personal situation
Prison, wall, bandage, and the lime.

Swing the emotion to the heroic pitch
Then whip the fleshy horse over the deadly ditch.

Cowardice

In journeyings my weak soul makes
And breaks the pestilence of swarming sin
I am the courier through the burning lakes
That bears the body with the message in.

I am the field of war, where good and bad
Mingle and batter and break, striving for place
Like well-matched warriors making an Iliad
Behind the fixed flesh barrier of my face.

Though battles and adventures over again
Possess this celluloid within my skull
Bones must escape the circumstantial rain
Blood must remain unspilt; flesh plentiful.

The play should stay in print, avoiding Action
Or else the text will suffer in translation.

Isolation

An isolated soul swirls round about
Discovering again its isolation
Its protestations make no connection
A whimper terminates its tapering shout.

Love holding out a hand clasps the indifferent air
The fragile virtues loiter, kick their heels
The vices self-abuse themselves: the body feels
About the heart the tight band of despair

Marooned. No better time to hear the voice of God.
You sit and listen. All of you tuned in:
Love rounds those faithful eyes: the Virtues nod
The Vices ever curious quit their din.
Knock, son of God, I am alone
And unentangled as a single stone.

Innocence

John Brown the Quaker weaver said
That evening sitting in my tent:
'I want a poem to have
Something to make me think
Over and over again and make
Me so much wiser than I was
The hour before I read.
I'm always wanting to learn.'

I wearing grey humility
As a suit of an imperfect fit
Thought, good John what can I say
To make you wiser than before?
I, the man whose vacant head
Has draughts of other people's speech
I, who amble through the streets
Collecting thoughts words deeds
To balance on a tray
Like knick-knacks made from scraps
The children use for play.

You who spoke softly to your looms
And looked upon the stars at night
On your way home from prayer
Now wait for God's sure sign
To draft you to another work
And His strong wind shall bear you
A lad from Burnley to the hidden East
To India, China, nursing calmly
Dark patients with excremental diseases.
Wherever you go your life
Will always be mathematically simple.
Across the criss-cross, the multiple
Tortuous tortured lives of thousands
It shall blossom like a bright parabola
Clean and narrow reaching the heights
And falling into heaven.

Apprentice Sermon

Out of this chaos of our life,
Love and anger, peace and strife,
Dream and action, pause and pose,
Mistake and motive, friends and foes,
Plan and impulse, saving spending,
Birth and death, beginning ending
Each in turn as he grows older
Attempts to put his house in order
Correlating this or that
Miserere or Magnificat:
Each according to his need
Fixes up his little creed
Carrying with him in his pocket
A railway guide, code, motto, locket,
Prayer and/or bank-book, policies
To cover his indemnities;
Maxims to endorse a habit
Like lettuce for a favourite rabbit.

But you dear, on the threshold still,
Have the unbroken fearless will
To go out walking in the dark
Exploring this unchartered park
Of hidden lakes and booby-traps
And pitfalls waiting for relapse:
Of hands that cling at your coat-tails,
To send you chasing up false trails:
Of dazzling side-shows that delay
Your schedule on the narrow way,
A host of friendly charming allies
Would have you shying at Aunt Sallies;
A world of effort and resources
Squandered on dark and dubious causes.

Not all our love or our well-wishing
Can save you from the job of fishing
In the unpleasant stagnant water
For the key of the dead hall-porter,

Nor can we lend but little light
To help you up the stairs at night
And only your fair hand can open
The several caskets of salvation;
And at our best we cannot sit
In your cold cage going down the pit.

I too have hardly ventured out;
My feet are blistering with doubt,
My compass swings from left to right
And fear corrodes my appetite.
As an apprentice who would learn
I unhesitatingly turn
To the first face in which I see
Reflections of the Deity
Gleaming through clear humility.

We suffer from the same complaint,
Humanity's distinctive taint,
And luckily you have at home
A specialist's consulting room.

In Philippi 2, verse twelve, we find
The sign-post for the wavering mind.
Now from the cross-roads far ahead
Repeating all the apostle said
Your father stands square on the road
Suiting the action to the Word.

Love then has an expanding sense
Wider in its full significance,
For from the world of ' you and me'
We can ascend perceptively
Towards the goal of unity
The unlocated particle, the tiny place
From which love vibrates life through space.

Eddie

Your squat familiar writing in the usual
Shade of blue tells me its author
Has sailed six weeks and crossed the equator
With troops to an unknown destination.
You, Eddie Thomas, bright boy at the County School,
Went out after matriculation
And six foot three passed months and years
In insignificant ill-paid occupations
Outside the orbit of the fixed professions.
I a vocationed youth used to visit you
Doing secretarial work, collecting rents,
Behind a counter, under shelves,
Each time bound to the iron calendar,

To the iron calendar that brought
This mechanised war and transcripted you
From the inhuman discipline of economics
To shouts from sergeants copied from the comics.

The bright boy never really went to sleep
But still in the security of the skull
He peers about through camouflaged eyes.
The iron calendar that grips
Your obedient body grudgingly now gives
Sweets to the convict soul and shall take you
With Vasco de Gama through new seas
And you shall see where the Israelites tramped the water
Or the Taj Mahal or the Ganges flood
And every book you scanned at school
Shall spring to life
Released by this conscription.

The Renunciation

From the hammock of his happiness he had seen
Three moving visions: the ageing man, the invalid,
The decomposing corpse. They had none of the unreality
Of daily living. They were thoughtful. They fractured
The glassy skull of peace.

Ten years he had lived
The usual happy marriage: the charming wife,
The perfect house, horses, the great career.
And now the crown of pregnancy the promise of a prince.

He was alone near the river
Dwelling upon a vision of a hermit
When a breathless servant came shouting of a son.
Single-mindedness like acid curdled
The impulse to joy: out of his silence he murmured
'Another knot to be undone'.
The pose for meditation, the stillness that could hold
The warring elements at peace was broken.
Slowly he went home. His body light from hunger;
His head a hive of thought; his heart heavy with sadness.

The village burst with bells.
They clanged announcements in the windless air.
Already the children were dancing the thin dogs barking
The maidens blinking in the sunlight the young men laughing,
And all ran out to meet him, the new father
The fortunate prince and tomorrow's kindly king.
Their noisy joy oppressed his head and heart.

But it was out of this shouting
A melody sung by a maiden won his ear.
The little cousin sang with persistent sweetness
'Bliss, bliss for the mother; bliss possess the father.'
Bliss he knew to be enlightenment:
Amid so much transient joy she wished him vision.
Her voice was the flute of wisdom. In gratitude
He sent her his necklace, saying,
'Let this be the little teacher's fee'.

But the noose of folly fell upon the maiden.
She giggled. Sadness returned to him.
He moved on.

                    There was such elaborate length
Such ceremonial weight to the day of rejoicing.
He kept the dutiful smile upon his face
While his eyesight blurred, and his ears hummed with fever.
Not until long after midnight did the whole court sleep
The solid sleep of celebration; and not until that moment
Did the prince send his charioteer for the horses.
Dressed for an expedition not a war he went up to the chamber
Where his wife and unnamed son lay sleeping.
The lamplight flickered as he stood and watched them
Among the flowers her delicate hand upon his tender head.

He knew well enough the tiny head contained
As a light bird balanced above holy water
The silver future hidden in a friendly tree.
There was nothing he had not felt or thought of
Until he was burnt to stillness by a last desire
Before leaving to hold the sleeping infant in his arms.
But he himself had decreed, beyond consolation
He should not embrace the power of his past.
The heart of human joy, brief fragile fallible
Was to be left in imitation of death

And so he rode away from the palace of illusion.

Page from a Diary

Crows in the rectory trees announce
Twilight before it comes
And I stand in the silent garden
Computing fruitless sums.

The air is scentless cold and still
The valley etched in colour
On a three dimensional canvas
Breathless and autumnal or

Like the reflection of a scene
In the still water of a pool
Whether of nature or of art
Calm serene impersonal.

Twenty-three are not enough
Years to crop the suavity
The chilling self-possession that
For art is a necessity.

Loneliness obscures the brain
Like frost upon a glass
Troublesomely aching the
Desire for happiness.

Now the birds are going home
Folding up their wings
Sleep like a drug relaxes
The limbs of living things.

Dearest, distant though you are
My imagination moves
Sea and mountain to one side
As though determined now to prove
The power of separated love.

Humble Song

Tonight, before I went to bed
Alone but reasonably fed
By an unfriendly hand,
A terrible humility
Rose like a temperature in me.

Then every word and every act
Seemed superfluous, inexact
And every thought like a lost sheep
Shivered before the impenetrably deep
Shadow of nihilist night

A numen lurking in the blood
Felt, feared, but barely understood
Suggested only this
Thesis, antithesis:

I am a sacrifice for all
That little children may grow tall
I am the murderer who waits
To shoot the prophet at the gates
A grain of cosmic sand
In an almightly hand:

Or in an unkown office drawer
My life lies waiting for
A clerk's impersonal thumb
My synthesis seemed true
From any point of view –

A doctor with his scalpel
Eyeing my tender navel
A nurse beside my bed
Grinning at what he said
And I lie passive, helpless stiff
Caught in an anaesthetic 'If' –

Tonight the wind blows from the East
Cutting the soldier's broken breast
Let each tear help to swell the flood
Washing away the map of blood
While I like any frightened boy
Clutch at my childhood's ragged toy
Running with heavy rooted feet
Down night's apocalyptic street.

In Brindisi

One would hardly consider Vergil lacking in feeling:
It was just that news from the East travelled slow.
One imagines that war then, like civilisation
Was beautifully local. Once perhaps in a lifetime
Men would fight in the valley, a few young bodies
Would be left behind like cut flowers.
The following day the heavy-footed clown
Would pass by hooing on his oxen, the
Squeaking wooden share scraping a furrow,
Turning over dried blood.

Vergil could sit in the wide shade of the beech
Comfortable with his tablets, considering
Hexameters and bees, watching
Out in the sunlight Italian children play.
The slave girl sings in the dreamy house.

He may have had a cousin in the East
Thirsty and groaning from dysentery and sword cuts
A sensitive young Mantuan longing
For the cool shade of the acacia, the fountain garden,
And a well-born woman's elegant laughter.

One would hardly consider Vergil lacking in feeling:
It was just that news from the East travelled so slow.

A Landscape in Hyde Park, July 1944

Here, the blind iron, engine stopping, struck
The now no longer house, blew up bricks
Glass, woodwork in expanding waves of dust
And left a heap of rubble. The noise subsided
And the sun resumed. Light burst
Through the stricken branches and ran its hand
Along the pale backs of blasted leaves.
The dead, the debris, the dust lay still in the sunlight.
The wounded pinned on the grass might have been acting
Or figures in a painting.
Small quantities of blood were spilt on this
Green carpet, and all the dead were strangers
Before and after to the living.

Now the same daylight falls on your sleeping face.
Your lithe live body lies on the growing grass.
I pore over your lips as a lover of books
In your library. I study the smooth lips
Pouted in sleep but able to open. O all
Of living latent in your body resting
The beautiful breath quietly escaping
Round breasts rising and falling I observe
Until I look up at the solid clouds and thick blue sky
And whisper 'This is the summer. There is no death.'

Song

Let us divide our days
With the diamond-cutter's art
With an untrembling hand,
Untroubled heart:

Our love calls for craft
Not spontaneity,
No accident of mood
No sudden gaiety.

Accumulated love
Like water in a drought
Must carefully be stored
And parcelled out.

Judas Iscariot

The honest saints found out your flair for money:
Your accountancy sustained the holy crew
John couldn't be bothered, Peter didn't worry
Who else could get the gold for God but you?
Much charity milked at the meagre coffer
Easter with all that food and wine, just emptied it
And so you sold your Christ for the best offer
Guessing he could escape from their blackest pit.

Such a shame you hanged yourself before that Wake
When he reappeared to dole out bread and wine
His cross to cancel auditing mistakes
His hands to wash your grubby silver clean again.
You could have wept with Peter, won not lost,
Watching the coffers fill and overflow at Pentecost.

Adapted from Gwenallt's 'Iwdas Isgariot'.

The Serpent

Like ivy climbing you wrapped your cunning about
The tender bark of the forbidden tree
Luring into its shade the naked lout
To sow the seed of Death in Arcady:
And away you slid, exultant, happy, hot
To spread your sticky poison like a trap
To catch his progeny: like the glossy knot
That punished Laocoon and the two sons in his lap.

In the wilderness you whistled after Another
And tried to hold him in your bold intelligent stare
But you in turn were transfixed. It was our Saviour
Who drew you to him, limp in the still air
Wound you about his body like a sculptured torque
To squeeze the poison from your lethal fork.

Adapted from Gwenallt's 'Y Sarff'.

February 1947

Over the frozen lake tired swans totter, sorefooted camels crossing the blistering sand; less elegant than geese, exiled royalty in an unfriendly country.

Rhododendron bushes that were cloudy islands in the lake water are now immobile shapes embalmed in ice, robbed of their third dimension.

A lightweight landscape smeared with frozen snow: the mountains a grim horizon, shapes of frightening age pressed against the leadened sky. The narrow plain is scarred with black woods, black hedges, and the foreshore is frozen.

A wave swelling out of the cracking sea bears broken ice on its crest to fall clashing on the glassy shore. On a white field a grey lamb lies stiff in icicled wool, its flesh stiffly freezing: the dead of winter.

Birth Day

Temporal facts abound: the humming clock
The snow outside, the throbbing echo of pain.
The sixth of February's seconds knock
Upon another door, another monarch's reign.
Unknown son, lord of a new minute,
Untouched by mother or father's sculpturing hand
Breathe in the immortal air, your wet eyes lit
To light immaculate, destiny still unplanned.
The night about your tender head shall flow
Like summer rain, the nurse's icy fingers
Discipline your wanton limbs, the small clouds glow
On the horizon, a choir to encircle you with singers
And now, without a yesterday in nineteen forty seven
You hold unharmed the golden flower of heaven.

Holy Places

The guide said, 'The earth is sensitive here
Often we have earthquakes. The rocks are soft'.
Miss Lacy crossed herself. 'He came down'.
She whispered, 'He came down and that
Is all we have.' She wiped away a tear
And we all crept out of the gold encrusted sepulchre.

Black Mount Ararat bobbed above a beard.
Wax from his crooked candle soaked his book.
Those glowing Armenian eyes were as indifferent
To us as the bold stare of a leopard in the zoo.

'To save us' is 'To save us' in any tongue.
I hear peasant harmonies in chapels, choirs
In unheated churches. I see dawn
Breaking out over the Powys frost

And a boy dressed as a king carries Christmas
In a heavy censer as he sings
His wounded sound. His lips are carved
Like a Coptic pharaoh's: is it a sneer or a smile?

'Here' said the guide, pointing to a post-hole
His voice too shot up and flattened on the roof
'Is the middle of the world.' And so it was.
He had no need to smile and bow. Half way
Between the manger and the cross

He had the cord about his neck
His mother's gift not the hangman's
And in our mouths the iron milk
Of her pity.

'Here,' said the guide, 'On this silver star
Our Lord was born among the pagan stones
And there,' he lifted the tapestry
Generously donated by the government of France,
'Beneath that grille and underneath that glass
You see the manger.'

Miss Lacy knelt and prayed and pressed her lips
To the unwinking silver star, to be nudged
Out of the way by an Arab wife, barren,
Wanting a baby. What else what else
On offer

'The Garden of Gethsemane,' the guide said.
The sceptic was unimpressed. 'Any old
Front garden. The olive trees are new

Quite frankly much as I would like to spare
Your reverential feelings, if these hills
Remind you so much of home
What you see is stone not bread
And the weight of the mountains
An accumulation of human misery . . .

Even from your point of view, Miss Lacy
The deposit of two thousand years
Of unremitting sin. If this is sacred
Everywhere is sacred.'

Miss Lacy grasped the seat in front
As the coach rattled on to Bethlehem
And her false teeth flashed in triumph.
'I couldn't agree more,' she said.

First Born

Washed up on a wave of time
Born on the sparkling new water
You open wet lips and breathe
The first cubic quantity of air

Unwind that embryonic posture
Lift a limp limb to the quivering eye
And through broken film, raw pupil, peer
At the sun dancing in the sky

As your skin tingles learn the texture of sand
While your untutored ear acquires
The first broken instances of sound

Pastoral Pose

I envy no one now:
The traveller who seeks
The side-shows of the earth,
The seven foreign seas:
The man of certain wealth
With mansions hid in trees,
The poet recognised,
The politician's scope
In human destinies.

I shepherd pass my time
Deploying on my pipes
The regiments of rhyme
Guarding the local rivers
As they flow in their separate courses.

The neutrality of summer
Preserves me with her smile
Boasting my independence
In an outworn style.

Coda

Hope germinates in stony places
Faith hides beneath the unturned sod
So that somewhere in a sea of faces
Love will stamp its image on an unknown god.

Pascal

Pascal, forbidding all to love him
With scientific honesty
Directing each to the self-existent
Eternal Deity,

Forbids each honest man
To cheat himself and others
Into a transient pleasure:
All men are brothers,

All women mothers
Who must wean
Children to a clean isolation,
The self-eschewing other selves
Selfishly seeking selfless emersion
Into the self-existent.

Such honesty I cannot face
Seeking my comfortable place
Among the pillows
Of the love of others:
The bed of roses
And the grave slipped into, accidental
Somewhere in the garden.

Romantic Illusion

She came like the breeze of a bell-bitten morning
Walking toward life among the quivering naked trees
A white dog at her heels, her thin robe
Ungirdled, free to sway about her subtle knees.

Her sweet image drew to itself the landscape
As the first star assembles the violet sky
The path she took stretched like a line of verse
To where I stood, and passed me by.

She was the jewel, the casket was Creation.
Willingly I would have been the road she trod.
But she breathed only the breath that made her
And when I followed she faded as twilight fades
Into the arms of God.

Interim Verdict

It is not necessary that you continue
You are not indispensable or absolute
Except for certain moments
When the sunlight
Is brushed by shadows of branches on the classroom wall
When light drops laughter
In that woman's eyes
And a damp wind girdles the tree trunk
And small sharp teeth sink
Into fruit that spreads its honey
Over little fingers
At such moments, prisoner,
Not recorded in the indictment

You may imagine if you will
That you are for ever
And that only in so far as you perceive do you exist
And that your existence is more and always more
Than the image of a victim
Racing towards the dark.

You shall continue. And continue for ever and ever.
Through you and never altogether without you
Others will go on stumbling through the mist
The fish will shudder in the deep-sea cold
The poet mutter, the insect shift under the cruel stone.

Partial Recall

Small as a top in the green garden
A boy fished for Time with a string and a broken stick
As if the breeze that stroked his cheek could harden
Or upstairs, after dark, the flame solidify upon its wick.

White-kneed cap-crooked in the sepia photograph
Before the War that put the sun to flight
He climbed the limestone hill, hid behind the gorse
And came down with a vision and an appetite

His mother or the maid did their best to stifle
With green peas, potatoes, meat or fish
On willow-pattern plates and on the bench outside
The loyal terrier waited to lick the sticky dish.

Childhood is conviction. The seeds of magic.
There must be places where these things are stored
Like dust between the granary floorboards or
Those ink smudges left inside the roller towel
Behind the kitchen door:

Enter the cave. There afternoons like bats
Hang black and leathern in the nets of Time
And on the sandy floor the dead in their dry hospice
Lie wrapped in soundless music line by line.

Rabbit Ensemble

Hearing the voice
Of my warm vocation I stumbled
Wishing to run up the slippery stairs
To my damp haven in the slender tower

Entering I found
A god-like rabbit nibbling my paper and
In the one warm corner his long-eared consort
Breaking my brittle pencil with the white tools
Of her hostile teeth.

Willing to thrust them out
Bloodlessly to inveigle two black rabbit-gods
Back to the labyrinth of their holy burrows
I was cunning, and bade the invaders welcome.

But as we sat talking
Of dentures and entrails and the price of lettuce
My impetuous head grew cold, my vocation
Departed, my ears were elongated and fur
Grew thickly on the back of my hand.

An October Day in Lleyn

Morning

In the brassy tavern above breakfast the dicer in glee
Lifts his metal leg as I this moment of morning
Sunlight (after the mild delicate moon
Last night) would wish to stamp
On the timeless my own configuration of joy:

Those apples, waxy, blushing
In the green silence: that bright bird
As it cleaves to a brighter sky, even the air
That shifts about the weathered boughs, and the mould
Of early morning caught in the soil in the sun
The brown grass where the black cat browses
And at the centre the young mother holding the world
As she casts the cord of time around the apple tree.

Afternoon

Afternoon of nothing trouble nothing
White edged as the running sea
Wrap our greedy hearts in singing silence
As the light lifts to bind up the wounded day.
Parchment heaven upon your unstirred face
I scribble a breath wrought image
And an infidel becomes a priest at prayer.

Evening

The sun must set. Westward the bay becomes a sheet of light
The water sucks the pebbles down the shelving shore.
It is too calm to feel the cold
The tide is harmless as an open door
With so much quiet nothing can grow old.

Governance

The governing classes
Embellish appropriate spaces
Their charitable purpose
To enlarge our
Limited perspectives

To be photographed
In yachts
Is not self-indulgence
They have lots
Of charities

To patronise
So never envy
Those perquisites

What they enjoy
They suffer us
To share
In coloured scandals

Their elders
Our betters in their villas
Before log fires
When the wind blows up
Dream of riots
Easily subdued

Ah the burden of office
To be spat on
By children in the street . . .
Memoirs like marble
Icons half hidden
By oleanders
Absorb sightless sunsets

Let us rule again
Empires of salt water
Obedient porphyry rocks.

A Subject People

We were the willing ones, the heroes in theory
Ready to risk all for the cause: now armchair
Guerrillas, house-trained politicians too wary
To leave unattended our heavily mortgaged lairs.

We are, we suppose, heirs of an inbred caution
Workers and peasants hoisted us into these better homes
However much our minds resent social distortion
The balm of compliance soothes the unease in our bones.

We have become a breed estranged from action
A chatty people of the more passive type
Savouring private feuds and sectarian faction,
We imagine disaster long before its time is ripe:
Here in our history's autumn we allow
The wrong performance and the evil bow.

Hugo

I was sorry to hear about Hugo. You mean Hugo?
He was shopping at Derry and Toms
Or pretending to be shopping, shuffling
From counter to counter, avoiding men
And looking for girls. What's wrong with looking for girls?

His beard was trimmed his collar washed
But his flies were undone. A curious oversight
We are all undone. Age has us in its grip.
There's nothing to be done. He should have worn a zip.
All the same a curious oversight
In one with his preoccupations.

His mouth was hanging open. What did he say?
Four letter words and bloody for example
Or some obscene display? He said nothing.
His mouth dribbled a little goodness knows
But there's no law against that.

A girl in a mini-skirt caught his attention
Her bright thighs flashed across his vision
And for a moment he was Phoebus Apollo
With one foot at least in the chariot of the sun.
Never mind the images. What made him run?

Nobody noticed him running.
His shopping bag bounced like a bow on the archer's back
Nobody heard him calling
Or his fervent prayer to the goddess but when
He grasped her knees mumbling they were marble
Chanting, invoking, choking with spittle.
The young girl screamed
And everyone noticed that.

Actors

X

Nothing about acting is easy: on the other hand
It requires stupidity to do it well and a certain daring;
Stupidity, that is, that animals display
When they repeat an action
With the mindless eagerness that is the source of physical grace:
A cat for instance stretching
To the same height against a door that will never open
Or an ewe turning to stamp her foot at an over-eager sheep dog,
Actions of patient defiance that can be repeated
From generation to generation
Whenever the situation recurs:
Be in touch therefore with your extremities so that words
Can fall from your hands and feet as well as your lips
Be a quiet gymnast let meaning shine
Out of your person like light from a lamp.

Seriousness is all to the good but learning
In the academic sense is useless
And so is the body-building correspondence course.
You take yourself as you are
As naked as you were born
And learn to steer the soft machine in flight
As if you were a stone skimming on water
Where the tide is time and each time you touch it
You are able to leap and sing.

Actors

Y

Consider an actor of fifty or pushing fifty
Who is still fond of himself, who still feels
The skin of his neck with a certain affection
Who still dares to use a reasonably well-bred masculine scent
And brushes his hair with the exact care due
To a greying veteran of histrionic wars.

Such a man has come to terms with himself
Rotating as he does on an axis of self-awareness.
Such a man has survived disappointment, insult, vilification,
Total misfortune and a measure of success.
And in so doing he has acquired a skill at handling himself
That is akin to the power of the old-fashioned seaman,
A knowledge of navigation as refined as that of a migrating bird.

He lives comfortably with his image.
He has lent himself to the imagination of his race
Advertising good looks, clothes, wine, tobacco and how to look
                                                    after women:
The lines on his face are the markings of a cultivated flower.

For this reason, when he stamps and swears on a rehearsal floor
It is easy to forgive him. When he has found his way into the part
And made it fit him, he will be calm and content
As a child after a meal
Will easily smile to show who ever cares to watch
That he is blessed with a full stomach and an unmalicious heart.

The Last Exile

A royal profile sulks into a pile of pillows
Sparse hair lies passive under a net
Her eyes make claims
Her eyes are never still

Her loyal servant that plastic earpiece
Has slipped
It dangles its faint distortions
Over the side of the iron cot
Near the bell she disdains to reach

She has come to rest in the white ward
The wheeled cot is the last vehicle

There is whiteness everywhere
And listening

The room is the length and breadth of a pause
And is closing in on the jaded pattern
Of programmes processed in a distant capital
The printed circuit of her heart's desire
The flutter of purple and rustle of flowered skirts
The ordered breathing of faithful clocks

The blood has drained from her ear
Her eyes are never still

She is repairing the cracks as they appear
With moist collects fragments of creeds
Ancient alphabets
But faster than she can work now
To restore the palace of her resounding past
The white pause is contracting

The Traveller

Possibile che a quarant' anni, e con tutto il mondo che ho visto,
non sappia ancora che cos'e il mio paese.

Cesare Pavese

His hopes weren't high – at forty how could they be? –
A meal perhaps, a brief meeting at the station
Or merely a telephone conversation.
As it often rains in the mountains, he bought a mac
But hoped for a glimpse of the sun.
Who sorted out the Alps? The train came first
And then they put up the mountains.

He had faith of course of the kind to make this journey
The destination seemed a fact of life. The wheels were oiled with
frankness
There was hope in the air but oblique as the evening light.
When the train slid in, the shape of the station was solid
The echoing shouts, the neon lights all seemed uchanged:
But when the strange voice said impatiently 'Who?'
Said 'I don't know I'm sure', and 'Who?' again and 'Where?'
It was a blow on the back of the head.
Not only the woman but also the place had moved.

His dreams were displaced. And worse. This was a loss of
existence.
He was less than when he started. A window-pane in the kiosk
Gave no reflection. The glass was colder than the ice outside.
His solitude had moved outside him. The world
Was indifferent as death to his pain and his pride.

'Who cares,' he said. Who cares?' He bought alcohol at the
station.
'Another train will carry me. The cemeteries and the cities
Are packed with the living and the dead. Somewhere in time
I may be recognised again and have my face touched by those
loving hands.

41

A dream is an adventure. The ski-lifts and cathedrals,
Taverns hotels cake-shops catacombs were never more
Than pictures in the magazine on which the matron in the corner
scribbles
Postcards to grandchildren stacked like sleeping prayer-books in
the homely streets.

'As for my experience', the traveller said. 'It was so long ago
It may never have happened: yet the human condition
Hardly ever changes. Everyone is punished for loitering
With or without intent.'

'Where to?' the booking clerk said.
He breathed deeply and it seemed to him he was displaying
exemplary patience.
'As I say,' the traveller said. 'Her moving fingers
Are a moving target. If she never existed how could she
Reappear so often? Did the lake at sunset burn
For itself alone? I tell you we were there.'
'Where to?' the booking clerk said.

'Don't misunderstand me, brother,' the traveller said.
'I don't pursue the thought, the thought pursues me.
And it's where I want to go. Can you offer a season ticket?'
The booking clerk screwed up his eyes. He had
Indigestion and a long day at the little window.

'There's a place,' he said confidentially. 'On every map
Where you long to return. Just give me the ticket.
I take the optimistic view. It may take time to find a way
But all I mean is where she is is where I want to go.
Don't misunderstand me. This is nothing to do with clinging kisses
Or the language of excited limbs. Those eyes are absolute.
They are a destination. Clouds open when she laughs. It is a mystery
And religions are founded on this kind of revelation
Not just memories to press between the pages of a book.
We may take a train to darkness but when dawn breaks
Mountains of faith and hope spring up all around us . . .'

The booking clerk screamed for the station police
And this is why they both spent the night in gaol.

The Duchess and her Duke

The day the photograph was taken
The congregation of tulips in the open bowl
Were well-bred and fleshy
The duke in profile smiled at the duchess and
The duchess in profile smiled back
Images were arranged as symbols
So that her candles carved elephants and
                waxed occasional tables
Mirrored his and those luxurious curtains
                free of dust
Divided in equal parts above the chesterfield
                they sat on
Divided in thick theatrical folds
And nothing in the picture disturbed a
                symmetry
As false as the two corners of a smile.

They were meant to be ageless. The time
Meant to be morning was light pouring from
                lamps
Youth bloomed in all the fabrics
Inside his shirt the duke was dissolving
In an acid bath of taste.

There was also the problem of the window.
The original showed the world and was removed.
Blind rectangles bolster their groomed heads
Teeth like polished stones hold open long enough
Their flaccid mouths. One twenty-eighth
Of a second was needed
For this deception.

The Colonel and his Lady

My armed man
Decorated for slaughter
His boots I licked
They aspired to rank
They arrived
He was first to the ridge
His eye blown out
He turned and hollered
'Where the hell you bin?'

Gilded with rank
Gold in the vanguard
Before a woman still
Young and breathless
He paid in full
For the palace mead

To administer death
In another country
He left me waving
On the summer lawn
A man goes forth
To seek his fortune
With seasoned troops
With armoured cars
With tanks at his side

In his frenzy
Mercy was frozen
He came to battle
In search of blood
In the ranks left standing
He flashed like a sickle
Among the green reeds

He was first to the river
As they say he took it
His sergeant was killed
Deserters were shot

In the bright morning air
They drove over corpses

A day for assembling fine weapons and armour
A day for advancing singing shouting
A day for destruction and a day
For the counting of corpses
Sharp axes sharp swords
Sharpest of all that day
In the minds of mothers

He licked my flesh
So welcome home
My muscular god one eyed
My sweating survivor
He will buy more horses
And a new Mercedes
The General insists
He must join his club

'At the rough ford
My best friends fell' . . .
Weakness enters
At night without warning
A man's wide heart
On lips still living
The battle song falters
On lips still living
The taste of death

At night when I touch him
I count the stars
My armed man
Sweats in my arms
Under his pillow
His teddy-bear hides
Ready to be touched
When he cries in his sleep.

Novelette

Mr and Mrs Cavendish-Cooper
How do you do
How kind of you to come
Never spoke to each other
For thirty years
Except in the presence of a third person
Cause and effect
Like a man and wife
When left alone
Lived in a silent house.

He took all the blame
That fatal visit
Prompted by boredom
To a Brazilian brothel
And the warm confession
Her eyes that wouldn't focus
As a result.

They gave famous parties
Filling the house and garden
Until they shimmered
In an alcoholic haze
Happy with gin
He told the parson
'All my life I've got on well
With every living soul
Except my wife

Women are strange and unreliable
You've heard the story padre
About two women in a wood
Who came across a tramp?

Property unlike woman
Is not violent
And goes up in value
You can understand my preference
My only daughter bless her
I always wanted a son
She sees her mother's side.

Well now she wants to marry
And there he is. I've got him
A failed B.A.
He owns a hand-made
Pair of shoes
And he's after my estate

But never mind. We talk
I know how to handle him
Such a lovely day
Can I get you another? The same again?'

His gin-flushed face
Fell into the flower-bed
All the women screamed
Except his wife.

Bourgeois Nationalism

Keep away from the radio
The morning is waving at you
And the birds are blowing
Benedictions and cliches

Close the gates. The top gate and the bottom gate.
Open your eyes
To the full infectious glitter
Of wall flowers and the power of weeds

Bring the argument to a close
With the white-haired English professor
Who hates the Pope
Loves the British Empire still
And worships mathematics
Stop him running about the garden
Shouting Progress Progress
And the individual doesn't matter
And it's all psychology really
Send him back to Staines.

Sit under the wall
Licking the wind and the weather
Study the sycamore leaves
And those impudent spruces
Grabbing more space
Sit under the wall
And wait for the cat to speak Welsh.

A Rural Man

A rural man. His battered hat shading his eyes
He opens his gate. On any day of the year he looks wise.

His work is incomplete. It never stops.
If he grins he grins at the sky not at the crops.

He has a wife. She does what she has to do. That river flows
Without his help. He stares and everything grows.

What signs does he read? What formulae
In woodsmoke? How hard does he try

To conjure out of imperfect fields a perfect farm
Behind those fibrous weeds an ideal form?

Meanwhile, in this space, unconcerned with infection, he spits
And under the hedge, unencumbered by time and place, he shits.

Two Generations

i. The Father

Those who fight and win are entitled to their reward
The service in the old style
A villa in the pines with a view of the sea.

Sit on the balcony and watch the sunburnt boys
Pluck the cones on the fir tree
Watch the judas trees cast their enticing shadows
On the pink garden walls.

At ten thirty the chauffeur calls in uniform
It is time to be driven to the riding school.
Above the lake there are yellow blooms.
My wife rides side-saddle through the eucalyptus trees.
The cook will do the shopping.

Tomorrow my friend returns from Mexico.
My broker rang from Brazil. That ivory horse
My son brought back from Hong Kong.
Three nuns visit my wife in the afternoons
To perfect their grammar.
I ride up-country to see my bulls.
The young men line up in tight brown trousers
To prove their manhood. This writer chap said
We torment and expel our bulls
As if they were reincarnated Moors . . . and I say 'we'
As if I were one of the natives.

No life is perfect. My wife makes friends
I feel obliged to hate. I walk in the cork forest
Until they are gone and think of the riding school
And my controlling interest
And worry a little about the country's affairs.

The Russians are inefficient. That is a comfort.
Maybe the Chinese will gobble them up
Before they finish us off.
Frankly it's machines I'm afraid of . . .
I won't allow them on the place.

In the evening let the maid appear
And circulate the oval table with her second load of French cuisine.
Let the old priest fall asleep before the fire
Let my wife talk of exiled kings and queens,

There are generations yet unborn
Who will admire my style and my reward
If I can make it last . . .
If they build that hotel block
To overlook my garden I tell you this
I'll blow it up.

ii. The Eldest Son

'There's nowhere like London! London's the place!
Admit it!' He nibbles his lip with excitement
Pushes his hair about and buys his paper.
It's going to rain, but he wears no mac
There are holes in his shoes and three cheque-books in his pocket.

The headlines are in his hands. 'Do you know
I stood here once about a year ago on a very bright morning
Outside Hamley's watching the buses and taxis
And thousands of faces flowing up and down
When I realised . . . I hadn't noticed before . . . A man in dark
                                                        glasses.
Standing right by my side. And do you know who it was?
Yes! Yes! It was Him! Radiant with promise
Perfumed with success. I noticed his shoes you know
Incredibly ritzy and a gold watch on his wrist and hair on his
                                                        forearms
Made for eternity or Pharaoh's tomb.

I said 'Hello' and he smiled. He didn't take off his sun-glasses
But he smiled alright. In fact he said 'Hello Buddy!'
I wanted to ask him without seeming oafish
If he'd heard of our venture, our Big Thing you know
And could I tell him a little about it.
Just as I made my first noise a chauffeur-driven Bentley
Drew up like a visiting ghost and whisked him away
Back to the Gods I suppose, those Elysian fields,
That charismatic platform between the stars!

That's London you see, anything can happen.
Governments fall and here you are in the same street
Reading about it! Great men die
And you stand here inhaling the perturbation
Sharing the tension with every heart that hurries by.

You can't be informed by a garden. Or buy newspapers from trees
I'll wait for the next edition. It's got to come out . . . It's got to!

You stand here long enough and History becomes
Someone you've met. There are shreds of wealth in the air
And kingly music, fortunes won and lost
Love reflected in every window and in the sky
Images of scandalous women elevated
By our breath their backs their buttocks their breasts
Preserved in electric milk and all day long
Although *you* cannot hear it, everything is singing.'

Hawkins without a Number

Hawkins. He had a lesson to provide
On the retention of urine
Toothless unshaven he slipped through
The regulations like a snatch of sound
Through a keyhole
Or a bubble in a water pipe.

He stood in the middle of the cell
Between his cot and mine
Scratching his head and muttering
The screws. They think I'm having them on
But honest to God I don't remember see.

You say something and I take it in
And then I blink and I've forgotten it
And they don't believe me see. So what can I do about it?

I've not got half my kit. That's for sure.
Are them your own teeth mate?
I've left my set at home. I can't do nothing with them.
What time is it do you know? There aren't no
Clocks in this place then? No I've not been in before
Ah well. If I knew the time I'd forget it
So what's the use?

He has a decision left. In his clothes
With his boots on. To sleep
He has forgotten to use the pot
But he snores more beautifully
Than a pig rooting about in
A forest of fallen leaves. Hawkins.

A Fanatic

What is a fanatic?
A boy asks who looks at the adult world
And wants to know.

Shall I say someone
Full of himself or full of a Cause,
Having ceased to distinguish
Between one and the other?

He drags his sufferings after him
He muddles his friends
And terrifies his parents.
He blames the police
Both for crimes and the law
He hammers the bonnets of cars with his elbows
He shakes his fists at the sun.

In the end he declares his love
For the comrades who betray him

And acts to demonstrate
The flame of his being becoming a torch.

The Sniper

Like prowling death he lurks about
The back streets of the shattered town, restless
As the sea is restless, angry

In his loneliness he longs
To fray the edges of the air

He loathes each glowing neck
That nestles in the coat of life
He aims to turn blood cold

He does not need as others need
A hearth a home a welcoming embrace
A voluntary smile

His satisfaction is the look
His presence prints on every face
The scream he barely hears

Their agony his joy. His skill
Selects another victim for the wall
That banks his solitude.

He never lingers. He returns
Invincibly alone
A solitary conqueror who thirsts
For more, his only dread
Extinction of this state of war.

Monologue of a Horizontal Patriot

The last train from Swansea. Just him and me in the compartment.
A lonely G.I. I said to myself when he offered me a cigarette.
A black wet night. I was lonely enough myself.
Back home in Detroit he was in the Bakery Business. Yes he knew a
                                                    little Welsh.
His folks were Welsh and spoke Welsh and went to the Welsh
                                            Baptist chapel.
It was a good business. Worth eight thousand dollars a year.
His uncle would meet him in Cardiff. Then there was silence.

He was going back to Munich on Friday. Big changes due
He said in the Army. New uniforms. Completely new.
Patrolling the Czech border I think he said he was.
There was another silence.

Twenty after, he said, we must be near.
We stood up and I said, had he liked Wales? and he said
He guessed so but, he shook his young cropped head,
It was a dying race.

                        And what did I say?
'As one Red Indian to another, or the hell we are?'
Or, 'we've had too much of that talk!'
I said nothing as I always do so now I insist
On saying it indignantly in bed.

                        We damn well refuse to die.
We are no more urgently scheduled for death than anyone else.
Listen you Welsh (I say this lying in bed) just listen
All of you, there's too much of this loose talk about this or that
                                                            dying.

Snap out of it frodyr, cymrodyr! We're alive
And we are staying alive and in our opinion
There is nowhere better and nothing better to be
(What do numbers count?)
On the shrinking dry islands of the world's swirling oceans.
Stuff that in your pillow. You knead it – pobydd. Goodnight.

At the Memorial

We remember wartime
Wartime
The leaves were red
Columns
Backs
Silences
Were broken
And skies were tight

Singers in uniform
Were frozen
Stony men
Were children
Nights
Flesh
Steel
Cracked burst buckled
Nothing was
The Target
Nowhere
The Retreat.

We managed
The living the key workers
The throats of loyal trumpets
The minds of washed out cockpits
Our prayers were pistons
We managed
Our leaders in bunkers

As indestructible as rats
The tongues and necks
Of true survivors

In one cold wood
A headless boy
Still walks
A thin man prays
In his own blood
The dead
On every side
Wait to be counted

Catalogues
Printed
In old blood

Old wars
Are not doors
They are the walls
Of empty tombs
Bowed to
At stated times
By true survivors
Only dreams
Have hinges

At the Bus Stop

As violins are about music
Her downward glance is about loving

A burst of sunlight is
An anxious benediction
Since the road is wet, the bus late

And the two heads of black curls
Impatient. They are twins
As eyes are twins

For her equal concern.
Up to a point only
Will she allow the east wind
To paint roses on their cheeks.

If I could measure
The intensity of caring from her eyes
To the top of their heads and the degree
Whereby the air trembles with
Tenderness between them

I would acquire knowledge
Deeper than the ocean bed
But the lights change
And the bus fills up the frame.

Bullocks

Our town is occupied by bullocks
Who are occupied by a nameless fear
And a throbbing need for grass

With a bull's horns
Fixed above their clownish faces
Their legs like hockey sticks
They stampede our streets

Sticky globes of innocence
Their rolling eyes
Can't read the rules
But they all run
Castrated their testicles
Are wrinkled like dried fruit

These were graded
Well-governed citizens
Of a consensus state
Situated in summer
Up to their knees in grass
Stuffing their large heads
Into honeysuckled hedges

In August their horns
Like television aerials
Were festooned
With creeping weeds
But gave no early warning

The rain seemed innocent
The cloud passed over
There was a stay of execution
And even a fleeting rise in prices
Before State Security unleashed
A lightning war

Columns advanced
Up country lanes
And the population was driven
All nostrils wet with fear
Towards the iron pens

No rescue is possible
In final solutions
Beaten and bleeding
Dispatch is crucial
No cruelty intended
They were driven all sweat and shit
Into those tight pens

Stripped of souls
With nothing to save
They are units for slaughter
Not disciplined not organised
Too stupid to escape
They inherit nothing
Except the butcher's knife.

A Tree Waiting

A tree grows in its own time.
Stubborn and tender
Like caucasian miners, slaves of their devotion
Roots crawl between buried rocks
Loyal not only to each other
But to their green offspring
Paying their fees
For many summer terms.

That is responsibility. Birds
By comparison are frivolous. They squat
In their foul nests preening their feathers
Twittering about their rights
Celebrating in a riot of repetition
Their seasonal behaviour. Why should we
Marvel at their navigational powers?

Roots have to do with a system
But they are also signatures
Of a covenant, substance
Of a love that is native
Growing in its own time and its own place.

Poppies

You can assume poppies behind a yew tree are shy
Even though somebody put them in that position
You can assert their blushing red and the dusky bark
Is beyond a colour relation,
Has become an outlook on life:
But the notion is yours not theirs.

But what tells them to come back
And nod towards the yew tree?
They are not nodding. They are bending
And they do not protest that their black antennae
Are too delicate to comb:
But you can say if you must
They do have insight in their roots.

Even in the dead of winter, even under the snow
The seed of thought was there and in it
The latent welcome for the black fur of the cat
That will walk with measured care
Between the tissues of the promised blooms
And the weathered bark, according to instructions.

One More Dove

A paper bird spells peace
When it is white or cut out
With dedicated cunning from a cobalt sky

The neck balanced on nothing
Can point east or west
And need not mean surrender

A homeless missile of good will
If it should fall insert
That olive branch inside the damaged beak

And see it lift with the expectation
Of futures dealing in childhood
The securities of orchards
The consolidation of gardens

In the blind head of hope
One eye is planted as a means
To find the way back not as a target

Paper is less fragile than flesh
It can be cut it can be signed
White refurbished balanced on blue
More than an instinct for survival
Its neck reaches out of mind towards meaning
And has no wish to be severed or burnt.

Horses

Six horses on an open shore
With manes
White manes caught in the wind
Wild waves
White horses shod with polished steel
Sunk in the pebbles.

Like us redeemed
And given their freedom by a careless god
Like us they feel
About their naked backs the wind's rod
And their startled ears
The sea's persistent roar

Like us they see
A sunset where the first star wheels
Above the debut of the smiling moon

Like us they stand
Carved rocks of stillness
Worshipping the flood.

Turkeys in Wales

Tenders are invited for the supply of turkeys to County Council Establishments

Gwent County Council, September 13 1975

Certain turkeys survive
They believe in their exemption
Attribute
Their extra days
To the music
Of their eloquence
And their influence
With the Owners.

Their cold combs
Are colourless and flaccid
Their long necks
Shredded with age
Their feet are decorated
Like their feathers
With fading orders
And birthday honours.

They consider the stony field
A sphere of influence
Or at least
A corner of comfortable exile
Reserved for their survival.

The hungry young
Observe them
And the brightness of the seed corn
Those tireless beaks
Gobble with horny care.

Such birds
They whisper among themselves
Consume the last lumps
Of our sunlight

While comrades in fresh feathers
Are snatched
And sacrificed

If we had hands
We could learn
To turn
Necks into wreaths.

Director with Star

Clear the piazza! I want
A marble chess-board to give her standing room
The last piece left untaken
Not quite naked but still
A product anybody could eat

I have snared the Duomo
In a network of flying buttresses
But she evades my capture

And I hide red eyes behind dark glasses
And yearn for the gift
She declines to give

She will escape into the sea and the stillness
While I paint the scene
On the inside of my skull

At least I can drag frame after frame
With a claw of hope
So that my machine will transform
Her smile into cash
With a gravitational pull.

A Chilly Morning in Oak Park

Paris, London,
They were never Athens or Rome
And they've lost the inclination
To preen themselves. Never mind.
We'll find a space for them
On the shelves of the Natural History Museum.

Thing is when you exercise power
You put bits of the planet like Indians
In Reservations for their own good.

Nobody is saying History is bunk
But millennia have to draw to a close.
What matters now is what happens
On Southside or even Little Rock.
Caesar is dead and the Tsar
Sleeps with the Kaiser but
This chilly morning a future President
Could be conceived in Oak Park

And he will talk about United
Nations along with States in expanding terms.
It's a swell notion
To rid the world of ethnic rubbish:

Because the Frontier will always be
What matters and expanding power
Be friends be folks be fellow Americans.
There are galaxies waiting for your hungry hordes
All over the skies real estate for the taking:
Politics dissolve in an abiding duel
With the stars.

Overheard at O'Hare

There's folks
And there's friends
And there's people.

Folks you gotta have
Friends you can choose
People are all over

With folks sometimes
You have to pick up the check
With friends too
If they're worth it
But with people Buster
Never

You can be polite
That don't cost nothing
But keep it short
Remember time's money

And you watch out for guys
Who say 'Thank you' all the time
They're after your money . . .
Where's that goddam flight?

Petty Larceny

Those details
That belonged to you
Are now transferred
To me
But in the process
They have lost
Their bright autonomy

Like slaughtered flowers
They cannot bloom
With even transient
Power
Life's revelations
Live and die
Within a shrinking hour.

But pressed
Among these pages
A perfume is
Concealed
And through the force
Of fiction
Another life revealed.

The Farmer's Wife

Tell me
    Tell me said the farmer's
Wife what makes a poet
Apart from
Breaking up lines? Do you
Have a licence? The wild vine
On the granary wall scrawls
Free verse without being fierce.
Feeble sneer: who
Can read weeds?

Can you squeeze poetry
From these arthritic fingers
Or maybe my feet
Ankle deep in dung.
Send me nymphs, Timasarchos,
To dance in the pigsties
And keep their feet dry in court shoes.

Birds come and go like poets.
Afraid of the seasons, escaping
On emotional thermals, caught, wrapt
In self regarding flight
All ephemeral music.

You are children, she said, playing life
By ear. I see you plucking at wet pages
Printed outbursts trapped in the hedgerow
Why not try ogam? Scowl
In seasoned stone.

I tell you lines like seeds should fall
In a fragile furrow. Time must have
Its way. And in the snail's race
As you grapple with the toils of toil
The canticles of fruition will provide
An extravagance of canons and inversions.

Friendship

A steak from Waitrose
Cooked in butter on the basement stove
Wine at seven and six a bottle
New potatoes on blue majolica or were
Those wide plates made of glass?

You fingered an old diary on the table.
1954. 'Not a good year for me
So let us like Wittgenstein
Pass over in silence
Not so much the things of which we cannot speak
As bloody unspeakable things . . .'

It seemed intensely witty at the time
There was blossom on the lilac in the garden
And chinese tea leaves in the sink.

Those were the days. And of course they are long gone.
You have your silence and I nurse
This flickering hope that skulls have other sacraments.

A White World

In the white world of heaven nothing
Is left to chance. Ghosts
Sit up in bed where
Floors no longer exist and thoughts
Are arranged in flower pots

To be contemplated until
Petals fall into space
Like library novels and settled accounts
Quilted in autumn colours.

Everyone you ever loved
Are fingers stretched on sloping harps
Polyphonic harmonies fill
Space like an everlasting sunset
Or a mile high tower
Without foundation other than
A grace note of awe.

Aspirations more potent
Than sperm permeate liquid forests
The progenies of guilt shed all

Their sins like pollen and in
An endless hive of wonder renew
The architecture of innocence.

Was and will be are one
And eternity smiles as she nestles
Inside the feathers of her home-made second.

Ancestor Worship

i

The dead are horizontal and motionless
They take less room
Than the stones which mark the tomb

But the words they spoke
Grow like flowers in the cracked rock

Their ghosts move easily between words
As people move between trees
Gathering days and sunlight
Like fuel for an invisible fire.

ii

Grandparents whose portraits hang
Like icons in our hearts
Carved out acres drew up codicils
To brace out lives
But the new estates cover the fields
All the names are changed and their will
Is broken up by sewers and pylons.

iii

Our remote ancestors knew better.
They were all poets
They all wove
Syllabic love into their wooden homes

They saw the first invaders come
Pushing their boats through the water meadows
Their teeth and their swords glittering in the stealthy light
And they carved metrical systems out of their own flesh.

iv

The air is still committed to their speech
Their voices live in the air
Like leaves like clouds like rain
Their words call out to be spoken
Until the language dies
Until the ocean changes.

Poet of the Old North

E bore duw Sadwrn cad fawr a fu —

Saturday morning a great battle began
Blood shed as long as the day lasted

Their mouths were filled with earth
But his words were not wasted

It was more to him than a demographic swing
The barbarous thrust more than an ethnic threat
Covered with classroom notes his verbs
Are bloodstained faces.

Four hosts led by the Destroyer attacked from the east.
The warm kingdoms summoned their men, the training feast
Was foregone. Out of the silence burst the voice of the Blusterer
'Send your hostages forward
Send them dressed in the garments of peace
Call me Overlord call me master
And from this day our conflict shall cease . . .'

Unreproducible blunt repetitive rhymes
Like the breath in his lungs
Made short and immediate by danger
The last moment the culmination of times
Of postponement. The cold future hangs
In the air while the nation waits for the leaders' answer.

Owain son of Urien in the vanguard
Made the first reply. So proud of his descent
His voice was the first blow. 'There are no hostages

There will be none. Today or any day.'

Then his father spoke, Urien, Taliesin's master,
The great lord of the lakes, the leader of the host:

'They wish to meet us! They have proposals to discuss!
Make a fence of linked shields! Let us
Show them our faces over a rim of steel. Let them
See spears level above our heads! Let us
Fall upon them and pick out his head
From their ranks as they tumble
In heaps before us.'

And there he pauses.
No account of the battle is given
Only the scene at nightfall

Before Llwyfain wood
Between the hills the site forgotten and the country lost
The corpses have stopped bleeding
But the gorged crows are daubed with blood.

What does *armaf* mean?
Armaf arfaethu, paratoi can?
– *virumque cano* – Push the letters about
Split the syntax, change the language

The voice of the poet fits
His cattle on the narrow bridge
Defy the passage of time

As the little scholar said
Old deaths are the latest

Take a year take a lifetime
To hammer out this song.

A Roman Dream

The dust of the chariot race is in my hair.
I hide under the laurel bush like a piece of silver.
The guards use ferrets and before dawn they will find me.

Last night the Emperor painted his face green,
We all agreed this was the correct colour.
I was a little drunk. I agreed too much.

His god-like gaze discovered me,
An academic working on his uncle's prose.

I have long admired your style, he said,
But recently I find it makes the content suspect.
Come with me.

With green lips he kissed the short sword
And put it in my hands
With green hands, he exposed the prisoner's ribs,
An unknown prisoner whose face he said
For my sake had been covered.

Here, he said smiling. Here. Between the third and fourth ribs.

Push.

Push.

Whose face was beneath the napkin?

Push.

I wish to be loved by all men
I have spent fifteen hours a day
On Odes to be admired
In addition to my academic work
My research
My teaching duties.

Push.

My contributions to enlightened journals
On the balance of ambition and duty to the state
On the rational content of the Imperial dream
On human dignity

Push

On precision in syntax
On language truth and logic

Push

His royal hand, soft and perfumed, closed over mine
With childlike suddenness pushing

The warm blood hit my face

Sounds came from my throat like vomit

The faces of gods are green, he said, not red.
Would you agree?
I nodded and I nodded.
Will you die for me?

I don't care what you choose but make the choice your own.
Fall on this sword like a Roman
Or swallow poison like a talkative Greek.

The air was cold as marble.

The green god was bored.

Or run to hiding like a rabbit and my guards will hunt you . . .

If I could get to the hills
Somewhere in Tuscolo beneath my teacher's ruined villa
There is a hiding place and a secret spring.
If I could find the strength to make the journey
There is dry blood on my lips
The dust of the chariot race is in my hair.

An Apple Tree and a Pig

Oian a parchellan, ni hawdd cysgaf
Rhag godwrdd y galar y sydd arnof.

i

All men wait for battle and when it comes
Pass along the sword's edge their resilient thumbs.

Men clasp in faithless arms their sobbing wives
Testing even in the salt kiss the bliss pricking points of knives.

Men clip on armour and see in their children's eyes
Their swollen images, their godlike size.

Men assemble together, create a new sea
That floods into battle. Men become free

Of the dull bonds of life, become locked in a fight
In love in league with Death, lost in icy delight.

ii

In such a frenzy I slaughtered my sister's son.
My sword cut open his face and I screamed as though I had won

Glory to nurse in the night, until I turned and saw
The flesh of Gwenddolau, the young king who loved me, raw

And Rhydderch's sword dull with Gwendolau's blood
And his great mouth trumpeting joy. Ah then I understood

That rooted and nourished in my own affectionate heart
Was the spitting devil tearing our world apart.

iii

When I fled to the wood, alone I lay under a tree
Still hearing the clash of our swords, still dumb in my agony.

So much despair had crowded into my heart
My tongue was cold, speech a forgotten art.

As I lay in the wood I suffered the germ of peace
To penetrate my veins like a lethal disease.

iv

I have lost all desire to communicate with men.
My sighs do not disturb the building wren.

An apple tree and a pig: these are my friends
With whom I share my wisdom that no longer pretends

To be wise, since nothing my wisdom brings
Can restore the lost kingdom or challenge the armour of kings.

I have eaten the apple of knowledge and all I know
Is that love must fail and lust must overthrow

And in the nights of winter when the ice-winds howl
A pity and a terror fasten themselves on my soul

And I cry upon death to wrap his white redress
Without mercy about the stillness of the merciless
And remedy my madness with long silence.

Dialogue in a Garden

We sit and talk like subjects of a dream
In a garden where the five senses
Float in five personifications and we remain
Sitting in deck chairs moving mouths
Moving the mouth-piece of the dreaming brain.

    And you ignore the pipestem stuck between your teeth
    Tobacco smoke that blends with other smells
    The declining sun, my voice that cuts the evening air
    In this seclusion far
    From the unreality of war.

Have I not lain on a tenement roof at night
And watched the sky turn into a battleground
Death dropping from the engines in the sky
Fiercer than molten lead poured down the scaling ladder,
More mutilating than torture.
I have walked a suburban street like Abednigo in the fire
And stood, alive among the flames of death.

    Yesterday I bent my back
    And thrust a sharp spade through the soil
    Ate meat and potatoes for dinner and went to bed
    Smoothed with the pleasant ache of toil.

Toil . . . work is a protracted dream
Body and Mind circling in the half-conscious.
Life comes to life near death.
For many days and nights I stood
At the crude operating table seeing stripped bodies
Poised between Life and Death

    I have buried dead lambs with keen regret
    Throwing earth over wool, stamping on turf
    I straighten to reflect
    Enrichment of the soil and future glowing sward
    And look about at sheep nibbling the rising grass.

Once in a smoke screen we attacked
Threw ladders on barbed wire
Ran shouting to attack
When others dropped, bullets passed or stopped,
I ran on to achieve the trench
My bayonet reached its goal
Twisting in a foreign belly.
Strange intimacy;
I remember ecstatic dying eyes seeking mine in gratitude.

It grows cold: shall we go inside?

Dream for a Soldier

First thing after breakfast I'll ride out
Into the spring, and the dazzling sun
Shall glitter on the sliding river, and break
Munificently through bud-broken branches
I'll ride out as innocent as the young morning
Ignorant as a wish, with no ulterior motive
And almost as though by accident we shall meet
And I shall kiss you 'good morning'.

We shall go on together. Perhaps we shall sing
Our voices blending naturally with
The cool music of an isolated thrush
And water falling among rocks.

We shall pass a blind man and two brown horses
Harrowing a stony field, and call out
'Good morning, brother.' He will smile
Without seeing us and wave with an uncertain hand.

The road will pass through a wood; a cock pheasant
Will march like a guardsman through the tall bluebells
On to the road, but rising at our approach
Obliquely on whirring wings.

The landscape will not be new but lovably familiar,
Hallowed by a past we cannot remember
The fallen wall, the ruin, and the incongruously leaning boulder.

As we climb dead fern shall crackle under our feet
The heavy smell of gorse in the sun shall assail us
And where we rest, clean and cropped like a lawn,
Private as a park among the rocks.

This day shall move as a symphony
No less enchanting as its end approaches,
Crossing the fields, the fence adorned
With a carrion crow and the pinned out pelt of a weasel.

The sun declines. Withdraws with enormous grace
A dumb flourish in the minor key.

We shall be unarmed and harmless as doves
As we wander slowly homeward, towards the house
Where the seven deadly sins are locked in a book
And O how beautifully tired and simple
Our prospects of rest as we stand by the window
Watching the twilight assemble

Miraculously unaware of the horror over the hill
The stricken village cold faces and hot guns the military thunder
As we lay our unblemished heads on a common pillow
And sink like gods into a wholly selfish dreamless slumber.

On the Death of an Old Woman

The doctor gave her three months.
Always economical she took two.
Only daughter married, living far away
Her life wound up, what else was there to do

Except lie still in a cottage hospital bed
Have faded visions between bouts of pain
Swallow so many teaspoonsful of gruel
And throw them up again.

Her brittle belly could hold nothing down.
The nurses fed her lightly to keep her clean,
Ate the small bunch of grapes the vicar sent her
And drank the quarter pint of cream.

Her last few days of life were rather a problem.
Ethically, we considered, was she of any use
No family, no hope, a wasted body;
The question was abstruse . . .

O biblically stripped of all protection
A rotten seed sterile of further production
No power in her withered hands, breasts dry
And shrunk, a failing brain,
Belonging to no one, and by no one claimed;
The woman had no function.

Every remaining day she lived
At the community's expense
Preserved in secrecy
To avoid offence

To the thriving world outside
The lusty business of living;
To them her futile presence would have been
The scarecrow criminal hung on the windy hill.
She would have caused politicians to shudder
Soldiers to cry and film-stars to fall ill.

At the Frontier

Six drunken soldiers at the barbed-wire frontier:
From the beer, gin, whisky, rum, churning in their bellies
Fumes swirl like incense into their heads.
They stare with bloodshot sullen eyes and blink
At our steady sober headlights. Resentfully
They call out for our passes, curse at us
For our cold intrusion. (My lights
Are the parson's book and the sexton's bell.)
Fumbling around, armed and dangerous
They frighten the women and make the men uneasy.

These, we think, are six beasts, made bold
With bayonets and guns, drunk not only
With liquor but also with an illusion
Of power for life and for death.

They would willingly shoot or stab, we think,
At the slightest provocation, kick a woman's ribs
With a bully's hob-nailed boot, mutilate
A corpse with animal pleasure, view
Blood with stupid fascination
And grunt with a primaeval exultation.

We hate these men as we wait in the dark,
We resent their indecent portrayal
Of what we dream or know lies in ourselves.
An honest comrade mutters, 'There but for
The grace of God, go I,' and all are profoundly insulted,
Horribly disturbed.

I think we would view their execution
By guillotine, or chair, or rope, or bullet
Each of us has his private preference, his *bête noire*
With a cold satisfaction or perhaps,
The more sensitive, with the vague pity we expend
On an old dog or crazy bull being shot.

At two o'clock six drunken soldiers staggered
Vomiting and cursing, off to bed, collapsing
On straw palliasses, sleeping as they fell,
Arms out or legs bent under.
Some moan like frightened children in their sleep:
One sees a childhood devil; one an enemy;
Another sees Ma in the little kitchen baking scones –
Her cracked and soapy hands on washing days;
An awkward kiss in the alley, the girl ran home –
The smell of a hay loft in autumn – the smell
Of a dung heap being turned on a frosty day –
A beaten wife's deliciously unwilling love –

Six drunken soldiers. Tomorrow morning
Comes the biliously green dawn
The agonising yawn, the half-hearted curses.
The youngest will say, rubbing his
Stupidly wet soft mouth – 'The bloody hell I care.'

The Hermit

Everything that happens is a message:
Sleeplessness, stars out of sight, a misprint on a page,
The shape of that sack in the broken window pane.

I am fifty if you ask me but my age
Like my smell is meaningless. It measures
The air I have used, the decay in my teeth
And the walls of my hut. It is not the age of stone
Or even its strength that speaks to me:
Only its stillness.

She was never still. She wore hats
That made me laugh and scream. Naked
She made demands that turned me into a dog.

You may say I should never have married
And I would agree if it were of any consequence
But it no longer matters. The night she tore my arm
And spat in my blood she gave me
The sanctity of an object the colourless varnish
That preserves from diminishing contacts the glaze
That protects my human skin while those messages
Shuttle through the day and night and transform
The sores on my hands into crystal flowers.

I am a man made free. My hut stands
In the corner of a field. The rats run in the rocks.
The rooks congregate above me. My feet
Are wrapped in sacks my food is mouldy

But the foreshore is my kingdom, finding
Objects and listening to the waves I am
Collecting signals: the bones of a dead bird

A mollusc in a pool of purple water, sadness
A piece of wormeaten wood I am collating
A notation of the universe for the birth of a word.
I need my solitude.

My Great-aunt

My gloves . . . Thank you my dear. And my spectacles of course.
And where did I put my hymn-book? Oh dear . . .
Is it February or March? March? The first Sunday in March . . .
I must sit down a moment. A silly old woman I am
Yes I am. The first Sunday in March. The unspeakable weather
Turns mild . . . this muffled rain.

Seventy-five years ago my little sister died.
So long ago you may say, but it remains
Becomes more and more as I myself walk towards death
My fiercest yesterday. A dream recurring.
A dream I never learn to understand.
A simple death. A two year old with a teapot in her fist
Tumbles into the sexton's silence, into black rain water,
And no one hears her cry. I was seven then
And it was I that missed her. But the call and the search
And the anguish came too late. Father found her:
Mud from the ploughed field on his buttoned leggings
And his sheep-dog, Mot, sneaking unnoticed across the forbidden
                                                            threshold
He carried my sister, her dripping body, irretrievably cold
Into the warm kitchen and laid her on the table.
That is all I remember. They say he did this and that;
But I remember the unstirred pools about her little feet.

        One year later my mother died.
My father married again. A woman called Leonora.
Rather stupid. She used to say I was never 'on her side'.
When I was twelve the family was no longer mine.
I remember these things more clearly since your uncle died.

        There have been wars I know, and great disasters
A long life gains wide experience of weeping and tears.
But I have always been described as a cheerful woman.
I remember her last in her little coffin before the lid was screwed
                                                            down,
Washed and so neatly dressed, her face not unduly distorted.

I myself am on the edge of death and that is what
I remember
Because Time is nothing and as long as we live
We are liable to the sum of the world's sorrows at any given time.

My gloves my dear? I am wearing them you say?
And John, I mean David, taking me to Chapel in the car.
Forgive me, I keep on calling you John
My memory my dear. You know. Completely gone.
Now please don't either of you be vexed
I'm a silly old woman. Forget my own name next.

Uncle Thomas

His sermons were thick with symbols
When Elijah for instance mounted the fiery chariot
He dropped his cloak and this meant something;
When the alabaster box of ointment broke
The perfume was God's love filling the house;
A servant ploughing was more than a servant ploughing
An image always stood for something else.

His eloquence was measured.
His popularity greatest
Among middle-class congregations.
I know of a chemist's shop in Llandudno
Where his epigrams are still treasured.

He was a man of some standing in the denomination
He examined candidates for ordination.

His repertoire was full of loving images
And anecdotes that reassured
He listened patiently to children's verses
And told the sick that they would soon be cured.

At home he read philosophy in bed
His wife complained he never heard what was said.

Suffering from indigestion, old age and people
He told me once he found the world absurd.

Mrs Jones

There's a use for something every seven years, she says.
Always gnomic, she fills the leaking coffee pot with Indian corn
To fatten the geese that crop the orchard grass
And leave their wet droppings under the trees.

Her eyes glitter behind her spectacles
Like sunlight on a wild sickle like
The setting sun on mountain cottage windows like
Undeclared love.

A tuft of black hair waves from the mole on her chin as she speaks
Earlier her rage struck the flagstones her clogs
Woke up the serving maids her smile
Was a kiss and a curse her single words
Put pebbles in my cream.

Daily her energy drove us
Her words were whips
She managed machines and men:

But today, twenty-one years later her loving comes of age
It lives in this estate, this
Blossom of gorse, a sigh in the grass
As far away as horses in a field.

Gŵr y Rhos

There is no such thing as the image of a country
For this reason put up this flag for approval:
It is made of skin and stained with sunlight and tobacco
It speaks in pickled phrases the language of apples
And it is wide enough for a shroud.

It remembers the road as a track, pigs
In every sty, a railway running, a harbour
With ships, a quarry working, fresh fish, young people
And planting trees in holes big enough
To bury a horse.

This man is a king except
He makes his living emptying caravan bins
And uses English in the shop to avoid giving offence
To visitors who do not know
Where they are or who he is.

Pastoral

This morning, yawning, Dic Fawr said
'Evans the *Ship and Castle* is dead.'
'Is he indeed? Poor chap,' I said.

The huge horse rose in its shadowy stall
We smoked and watched its brown excreta fall
And Dic said, spitting , 'After all

You couldn't expect a chap like that
With bottles to hand from where he sat
Not to soak. His belly was like a vat.'

Dic went across to stir the horse's feed.
'Come on. Eat up,' he said, 'you're harrowing the fifteen acre field
All day today,' and wistfully to me, 'it was a nice death indeed.'

Outside the lark was gargling with dew
When Dic led out Captain, Belle and True.
The sunlight dripped in the lane. The sky was blue.

A Democratic Vista

Strange sanctuary this, perched on the rising cornstack
Like a desert saint on a broken pillar
Staring, eyes unstirring until hill field sea are one
The procession of thought blurred
Into the regular rising and falling of a sinewy arm
And the dry rustle of sheaves.
Tom Williams, Guto, Dick Williams, Wil bach, Dafydd Dew and
me,
We are the people; our conversation is smooth and superficial
Like a veneer of grained wood, curves leading nowhere
Which was where they started.
We are the people for whom politicians shout and soldiers fight
We sow and reap, eat and sleep, copulate in secret, think
In circumference of one dimension.
We are the sacred people, the secular mystery, the host,
Whitman's elastic deity, Marx's material, Rousseau's noble savage
Mayakovsky's beloved –
Tom, Guto, Dic, Wil, Dafie and me –
Reasonably efficient between dawn and sunset
God chewing tobacco, God drinking tea, digesting rice.
We are the people.
God is not mocked.

From Father to Son

There is no limit to the number of times
Your father can come to life, and he is as tender as ever he was
And as poor, his overcoat buttoned to the throat,
His face blue from the wind that always blows in the outer
                                        darkness
He comes towards you, hesitant,
Unwilling to intrude and yet driven at the point of love
To this encounter.

You may think
That love is all that is left of him, but when he comes
He comes with all his winters and all his wounds.
He stands shivering in the empty street,
Cold and worn like a tramp at the end of a journey
And yet a shape of unquestioning love that you
Uneasy and hesitant of the cold touch of death
Must embrace.

Then, before you can touch him
He is gone, leaving on your fingers
A little more of his weariness
A little more of his love.

Twenty-four Pairs of Socks

In the chest of drawers there are two dozen pairs of warm socks.
The man who wore them had the secret of living.
He was prepared at any time to say what it was
so that as far as he was concerned
it was no secret.

When he lived I could not think
that what he believed brought him peace and happiness,
was the true source of content.
If he said FAITH I remembered his ulcer.
Whether installed by heredity or induced by anxiety
an ulcer is surely something that nags,
coaxed to grow in a greenhouse of despair.

If he modestly implied GOOD WORKS by his concern for others
and his unswerving devotion to political idealism of the most
naïve kind
I would like to point out that he never cleaned his own boots
until his wife died
and as far as I know
no party he voted for or supported ever stood in danger
of being obliged to exercise power.

Sometimes his calm was unnerving
At others, one sock of a pair missing, or some such trifle
he would tremble and erupt –
the burst of red-faced fury
of an angry peasant cheated at a fair.

But mostly he was calm. Nearly always.
(Not counting a certain tremolo when he was swept with
righteous indignation.)
It was generally accepted that he was a good man,
and it pleased him deeply to know that his visits were welcomed.
In the wards his presence, his nod and bow especially,
did everyone a lot of good.

Everything about him suggested that the secret was not his own
but something given, something to share that came from a source
                                                    outside –
available to all like the warmth of the sun and words.

He was a preacher of course.
The drawers of his desk are packed so tight with sermons
they refuse to open.
His three suits of clerical grey hang in the little wardrobe.
In the chest of drawers there are twenty-four pairs of warm socks.

Master Plan

He bought stones first in the corners of fields
And thorn bushes for birds

He bought time like a lotion
To smear over the island in an amber light

He bought a master plan for the reconquest of the island
In such a way that loving bodies
Would not lie in the streets in pools of blood

Across the only bridge
He threw a language barrier

In the sea he inserted prohibitive sunsets
To change the nature of the invader

Growing flowers from the stems of their guns

He bought a tomb in the rocks
And invested all that was left in the stars.

Bron y Foel

The camera in the eye is personal
Limited in vision and partial
Signal and sensation
Storm through a human heart
To a selfish pencil

To see or to be seen
You face the sea and the sun
You face the West
Feet planted firmly
On the rock of Moel y Gest

At Bron y Foel we shall relax
Where hot Sir Hywel hurled his heavy axe
Amid the disturbances
Of his private spring

And share the landscape
Of our promised land.

Bron y Foel – a fortified manor house associated with Hywel y Fwyall (Sir Hywel of the Axe) a turbulent warrior who gained his fame in France and came home to a life of interminable disputes with his neighbours.

Nant y Benglog

Nothing new
Since the glacier slipped away
A lake of thin blue water
Never more than ten feet thick
And boulders
In a frozen queue
A river of stone
Down the side of the scratched mountain

Nothing new
A patch of pasture
Punctuated with stones
Black cattle
With short legs
Reflected in the water
Birds from the sea
Inspecting the mists

Nothing new
In the valley of skulls
A stone pulpit
Where ministers preached
In the open air
And stones became bread

Nothing new
Except coloured anoraks
And J.C.B.s
Moving slices of landscape
To widen roads
Increase lay-bys
Multiply parking space

Nothing new.

*Nant y Benglog, valley of the skulls, once remote and numinous,
and now bisected by the A5.*

Betws Garmon

Places need people
But not too many
Figures in a landscape
Pose with respect
With studied calm

One boat on that small lake
One lonely fisherman
Who sometimes whips the water

Not too many sheep
To count on the slope
In the sudden sunlight

Other children playing
Smoke from cottage fires
Not too many clouds

When places love people
Mountains are messages
Stone words against the sky.

*Betws Garmon – the beadhouse of a fifth-century saint.
Celtic hermits favoured remote sites and isolation. Garmon,
however, is cognate with German. So there is no need to be
exclusive. All that is asked for is respect for the place.*

Traeth Neb

No beach is truly private
On a wedge of sand
Thrust into the estuary you love
Among the dunes
And facing south
He built a wall
And inside his private house
With a twelve-month garden

Stocked with plants
To give him pleasure
While he wrote
Sarcastic memoirs
And savage notices
For distant publication

At low tide
The outline of buried cities
Showed above the gleaming water
At high tide
He did not hear
The buried bells

When the storm struck
The dunes moved
The bells rang out
The house became his tomb

The waves returned
With a shy advance
Birds from the hills
Joined the oyster catchers
On the edge of the tide
No beach is truly private.

Traeth Neb – no man's beach. A cautionary tale. The moral would be 'beware of legends'.

Mynydd Bodafon

This is a complex mountain
Older than the Alps
Worn down with keeping
The Harlech dome in its place
The boss of our island shield

We must show it respect
Take off our shoes
And use the path like a carpet

A cloak of heather
Hides the northern side
From the wind across the sea

But facing the mainland
The old outcrops frown towards Arfon
And warn the stone tents
Of an army of sleeping mountains
Never to move.

*Mynydd Bodafon – hardly a mountain, but a granite pre-Cambrian
hill in Anglesey solid enough to dominate the mountainous mass
of the 'Harlech Dome', as the rocky centrepiece of Snowdonia is
known to geologists.*

Llys Dulas

The tide has left a mirror on the shore
Into which the sky can smile

The lady of the manor
Long since dead
Built a refuge on the rocky island
And left food and drink there
For any shipwrecked mariner

But ships for us
Are toys on the horizon

And only rats live on her island

The lady of the manor
Long since dead
Built a dovecote
As beautiful as a baptistry
To be reflected in the tidal mirror
But there are no doves

And only rats live in her dovecote

The house itself among the trees
Is now decaying
The minstrel gallery
She had built with love is broken
And from the music room
Comes the cackle of caged birds

That from time to time
Are also attacked by rats.

Llys Dulas – a decayed mansion visible across Dulas Bay. It once played a notable part in the social life of the island.

Din Lligwy

Did they ever have time to garden
I mean the builders of this village fortress
Four circles a square a rectangle
And maybe a defensive wall

An old woman sleeps on straw
Outside the stone hut
And sees Orion's belt
A glittering bracelet
Above the tops of the trees
A bracelet lost on earth
But found again in heaven

Between the nervous watch on the sea
And the feverish hunting
Did they grow flowers

A thoughtful man from the hut circles
Ventures alone to the deserted beach
Unarmed except for a stick
With this he touches a jelly-fish
As big as a shield
He scars it with his stick
And mutters 'to be so cold
And still to be alive'

Four circles of stone a square a rectangle
Dead like the ghost of a leaf in a dying fire
Someone has planted daffodils among you
And in springtime they are flowers on all your graves.

Din Lligwy – the limestone ruins of a fourth-century fortified village. A crude attempt to give a Roman shape, we are told, to a defensive position nervously overlooking the bay. In the spring the site is surrounded by daffodils.

Hen Gapel

On the green headland
A single ruin stands above the sea
In spring it seems the skylark's chapel
Because he soars above it
Weaving lanes of song
High into the well of heaven

In winter the cold ruin
Knows only the wind and the rain
Behind the thick wall
Half-starved sheep shelter
The hermit's cell is empty
The altar a fallen stone

We have counted the stones
And measured them
But nothing can teach them to speak
Except the skylark
When he rises again
Like a new prayer
To the presence of the sun
A high strong song
From a dried fountain of faith.

Hen Gapel – the old chapel. A twelfth-century ruin in the field between Din Lligwy and the sea. It has a tiny underground shrine that children call the hermit's cell.

Traeth Bychan

Love easily finds its way
Along this rocky shore

And the blue of the sea
Is easily reflected in her eyes

The path is practised
To receive the footsteps of lovers

In the wild hedge
The flowers offer themselves
To lovers' hands

Distress and disappointment
Like the salt on the wind
Are widely dispersed

The little waves
Are laughter

And at the water's edge
There is a glass mirror
For smiles and reconciliation.

*Traeth Bychan — a secluded beach once favoured by lovers,
now surrounded by caravans.*

Cytgan

This is your country
These are your songs
Here live
A woman made of flowers
A bird that spoke
A man without a name
A queen of Ireland
Building her own grave

This is your country
These are your songs
Here we saw
A king asleep in a cave
A prince beheaded
A poet weeping
As the stars fell
Into the raging sea

This is your country
There are others
But this is yours
And these are your songs
Here we meet
Visions and preachers
Riding through the mist
Centuries like beacons
Fires on hilltops

Fire in Lleyn
And fire we trust
Forever in our hearts.

This is your country
These are your songs.

*Cytgan – a chorus. Not just, one hopes, a catalogue of
local legends.*

Pwyll a Riannon

Stallions greyhounds hawks and similar riches
Gifts he enjoyed from his former kingdom
The young prince shared with his men
And as they passed through the trees the meadows the parks
He gave a full account of all his strange adventures

They came to a hill like a throne a mysterious mound
Inside it was said dead warriors lay
Monumental with magic
And memory. Here we shall sit, said Pwyll, hold court
And invest all our judgements with respect for the dead.

This little hill has its own nature when it becomes a throne
The prince who ascends it shall enjoy
One of two things: a wound or a wonder.
Because you are many and faithful I fear no wound
But young as I am, I would welcome another wonder.

He made the mound his seat and even as they assembled
A woman on a white stallion
Appeared below the hill.
She was dressed in gold. Is there any way of telling
Why she moves so slowly who she may be or where she is going?

As she rode past the mound displayed its magic power.
The swift of foot sent to ask her name
Running as in a race
Never caught up with her. She seemed to glide
Unhurriedly but always out of his reach.

A horse was called for. She was still in sight
The way was flat and he used his spurs
But she kept her distance
And his horse, the swiftest in the stable
Could run no more. She was not to be overtaken.

They came again the following day. No sooner
The same number assembled than they saw
The same unhurried maiden
Nameless and beautiful. But no one could overtake her
By speed or by stealth. She kept her distance and concealed her
face.

She has a message, he said, if her stubbornness would let her speak
She will return and until that time
At the court we will shorten the day
With singing and a feast
Then I myself will pursue her and somehow break the spell.

But by no means could he overtake her. His own high-spirited
horse
Well fed as it was and playful
Never shortened the gap. Pwyll called at last
Young girl for the sake of the man you love whoever he may be
I beg you, wait and wait for me.

But gladly, she said, and for the sake of your horse
You could have begged much sooner.
She lifted her veil to release her smile
He was caught by her glance
And her image possessed his mind as from that moment.

May I ask my lady the purpose of her journey?
You may ask and I will answer.
My purpose is to speak with you.
You could not have journeyed for a better purpose
And now I may ask you why and you will tell me who you are.

I am Rhiannon daughter of Hyfaidd Hen
They wish to give me in marriage against my will
I want no man
Unless that man be you
I travel now to tell you this and hear your answer.

God witness my answer! If I had the pick
Of a world of fair women
My only choice would be you!

Very well. If that is how you feel
Before I am given to another man pledge a meeting place.

Any place in the world, he said of your choosing
And as soon as maybe.
This evening one year hence in my father's court
I shall see prepared a feast against your coming
Meanwhile live well and keep your promise in mind.

When they asked what had happened he spoke of other things
But when the year was spent
He set out with an escort of ninety nine men
They were well received
And all the treasures of the court were put at his disposal.

Places were set in honour for the officer commanding
The priest, the steward of the household,
The falconer, the judge, the groom, the poet,
The man who called for silence, the huntsman, the brewer, the
                                                                    doctor,
The butler, the porter, the cook, the man in charge of candles.
And Prince Pwyll himself with her father on one side and
                                                    Rhiannon on the other.

All went well until after the meal. When the revels
Were due to begin there entered a tall young man
With a princely air and dressed in silk.
He walked to the prince's table
And made his solemn greeting to Pwyll and his companions.

He was made welcome. Invited to join the feast
But politely he shook his head.
I am a suppliant, he said,
I must put my case. Are you willing to listen?

I will listen joyfully on a day like this said the prince.
Ask and if be in my power
Whatever you desire
Shall be freely given . . . Oh no! Rhiannon cried
You have gone too far you have offered too much . . .

His word has been given! Before men of two courts
Seated in honour. I beg . . .
Friend Pwyll said steadily state your request.
I want the woman you hoped to sleep with tonight
I come for her and this feast and these preparations.

Pwyll was silent. He had no answer he could give.
Be silent as long as you like she said
Your wits are on crutches.
This is Gwawl fab Clud a powerful prince
To whom they wish to give me in marriage against my will

Lady I did not know . . . Now you must give me away . . .
How can I? You committed yourself. You gave your word
He was speechless. Rhiannon whispered
Give me away and I shall so arrange it that he shall never have me.

How can that be? I have put in your hand a small bag
And you will guard it well. Me you can give
But not this feast which belongs to your men.
I shall promise to marry him one year hence

On the night of that feast bring this bag and bring your men
Hide in the palace orchard
And when the revels begin
You make your entrance in rags carrying this bag
And all you will beg for will be food. Enough to fill it.

It is in my power to arrange that not all the food
In three counties will fill it so that
After a while he will say
Isn't that bag of yours full yet?
And you will say until some mighty prince
Treads the food with both feet saying 'full' it will never fill

Whereupon I shall persuade him to do it and you
As soon as his feet are in
Pull the sack over his head
Tie a quick knot and put your horn to your lips
So that your men will appear and occupy the court.

By this time Gwawl was impatient. It's about time he said
I had an answer to my supplication.
As far as lies in my power
Pwyll spoke with a troubled heart
What is mine to give you shall have.
Rhiannon spoke. This feast is for those who have eaten.
For you, dear lord, one year from today
A fresh feast shall be prepared before you sleep with me.

Gwawl hurried off back to his kingdom. Pwyll
Went home with a heavy heart
But the year went by
And when the time came they were all in place
Gwawl and his men in the palace and Pwyll and his men outside.

In his heavy rags with his feet wrapped in sacks Pwyll entered
Just as Rhiannon had told him
Carrying the little bag. He gave
The solemn greeting and as custom taught
He was made welcome. Lord he said I come to beg.
Gwawl seemed ready. Now if your request is reasonable

As I am sure it is I am more than ready
That it should be granted.
Reasonable it is my lord. All I ask
Against hunger is that this little bag be filled to the brim with food.
Now I call that an unpresumptuous request Gwawl said

Fill up his bag. The butler first
The porter, the cook, the brewer, the man who made candles
And even the judge and the poet
Carried food and wine but no matter how much went in
The bag was never full.

Gwawl said as she expected isn't that bag full yet?
And Pwyll without smiling said
Until some mighty prince
Treads the food with both his feet
Crying 'full'! I declare this full! It will never fill

Great champion! Rhiannon spoke to Gwawl ap Clud
And up he got and in went his feet
Pwyll pulled the bag over his head
Tied the quick knot and put his horn to his lips
The court was occupied and Gwawl's men put in chains

And while Pwyll was stripping himself of his disguise
They invented a game
Kicking the bag and asking what's in there?
After each kick as he writhed they shouted 'badger'
This was the name of a game and a deadly insult
It is also another story

Prince, said the man in the bag, it would be most unfitting
For me to die in this sack.
Hyfaidd Hen, Rhiannon's father, was worried too
You should listen. He is right. It would be an unseemly death

I would welcome advice at this point, Pwyll said
Let me do whatever you say . . .
You will do this Rhiannon said before her father could speak
Let him agree to pay for his feast
And at the same time swear never to take revenge

You have an obligation to pay the musicians
Not to mention the cost of two feasts
Let him do this for you and if he swears
Never to seek revenge for this discomfort
Let that be all his punishment and set him free.

I readily agree said the voice from the sack
And as the legal arrangements were made
Gwawl stretched and rubbed himself and groaned for oils and
                                                           a bath
He left his men behind and hurried home
And then the places at the feast were taken by Pwyll's men

From the priest to the cook from the
Officer commanding to the man in charge of candles
And after the meal there were revels and singing and dancing
Until it was time to sleep and Pwyll and Rhiannon retired
To spend the night in peace and loving pleasure.

Adapted from Pwyll Pendefig Dyfed – The First Branch of Y Mabinogi.

Brân

i

Calm as green apples
Under the spider's thread
The kingdom of Brân

Brân
Emblem of one island
The strongest man
A giant armed
Blessed with gentleness

Bendigeidfran

As a rock that tames
The unruly seas
He ruled
His mouth
A hall of justice

He commanded first
Himself
His eyes
Were smiling doors

There was so much strength
In his arms
He held them still
And like the sun
He kept his distance

Under his royal shadow
Houses sheltered
Ships sailed
Into harbour
Between his feet
Unafraid
While his aura
Lit
The western sky

The world has one root
In the hand of God

The wisdom and the warmth
In the candle of his eye
I call the sun

I see the stars
As decoration on his swinging cloak
When he walks in the night
Of his own heaven

Order in his universe
His numbered balance
Of created force
Molecules of Time
Reproduce his harmonies
And in my peace
I hear them

From this rock
That He has made my throne

I court the beauty of the western sea
And the setting sun
I see my brother's chariot
Crossing a plain of water

And the flowers of another kingdom
Flourishing under the crystal sea

Sea horses glisten as far as my eye can see
And among them fruit and flowers, a stream of honey
To sweeten the mead of the second world

In my stillness
Both my kingdoms flourish
The salmon leap from the womb
Of the white sea
And the animals of God
Walk unharmed among the water and the wolves

Branwen's Starling

i

The sun was on his side
  The wind set fair, the sea
A cradle that would break
  A fall, while tirelessly

That clown among the birds
  Flew looking for respect
And under his warm wing
  The painful letter kept

The lesson he had learned
  Before the kitchen fire,
Perched on the kneading trough,
  Now part of his attire.

The woman's fingers worked,
  Her face a sorrowing mask;
Her skilful stitching bound
  His body to a task.

Alas! those gentle hands
  That once were smooth and kissed,
Cramped and captive, scarred
  Like two hands of Christ.

His burden is her woe,
  Her sighs must cross the sea
Under the starling's wing,
  A sister's misery.

ii

That day he started out
  As swiftly as a glance
Rising above the Tower
  He had no second chance.

Was it the hour before dawn,
    With frost thick on the grass
Or moonlight or the stars
    That saw it come to pass

    It must have been still dark
    The day he left her hands
    Before the morning bell
    Awoke the warrior bands.

Before the chimney smoke
    Announced the fires lit,
And brought the butcher boy
    Yawning towards the gate.

Already like a stain
    Across the unchanging sky
He saw the only course
    Her tears would let him fly.

Let the cold sea stay green
    And motionless as glass,
And let his seed of song
    Grow in the wilderness:

Until the hermit sun
    Emerges to display
Peaks and pyramids,
    The monuments of day,

And, like a rousing shout
    After long silence, shine
The mountains into view,
    Cold water into wine.

iii

Whatever time it took
    That journey from the earth
Into the nothingness
    Where myths are given birth,

The starling reached the land,
  He circled overhead
Where the shoreless seas
  Shrink to a river bed,

And searched among the throng
  Of figures in a field
For that one soul apart,
  A shoulder and a shield,

Like something sent from heaven
  To make the mighty wise.
He took him in his court,
  A giant for his prize.

One ruffle of his wing
  Brought her note to light,
But he had words as well
  To rehearse her plight,

How she was made to slave
  Above the kitchen fire,
Torn from her husband's love,
  Insulted in her bower.

Her sigh became his song,
  She taught him words, her name,
The message which he bore
  The flight that earned his fame.

                iv

What happened to the bird
  The legend does not tell.
Did he return forthwith
  To the sad woman's cell

Or sink exhausted there
  Unburdened, his abode
A grave upon the beach
  That Brân kneeled to prepare,

Or did he join the ship
   That led the vengeful fleet
Bound for the Irish shore,
And from the rigging call
   Each warrior at his oar?

The mast his stage, he plies
   Unruly parodies
A blackbird in the sails
   With thrush's melodies.

Their laughter never fails,
   Their smiles are bright like swords,
As though their world were free
   Of doom or tragedy.

Adapted from R.Williams Parry's 'Drudwy Branwen'.

The Young Warrior

A man's might
The body a boy
Ready for slaughter
All those stallions
Subdued
By his bright thighs
His smart shield dangles
Over their tamed quarters
As his clean swords hang
From his complicated belt
Of silver and gold

I say he inspires
Love not hatred in me
And I sing this
In praise of his young folly

Before a girl sinks into his bed
He will kneel in his own blood

Before the formalities of death
The tender laying out
The ravens will ravage him

This friend of the prince
Will end under crows

And shock will strike again
With the killing
Wherever it comes –
Marro's only son!

An Old Man Complaining

Before my back bent I was a bright talker
A story-teller an unique performer
With easy access to generous princes

Before my back bent I was handsome boasting
About my spear always first to draw blood
Now I am crookback cold croaking

Before my back bent my legs were bold
I strode into the great hall instantly included
A guest with a place of honour in Powys.

ii

Listen little crutch the spring has come
A cuckoo hides to do his grieving
Not one girl needs my loving

The summer is coming wooden crutch
The furrows open the shoots are green
And you manifest my weakness

Wooden crutch I think of harvest
The fern stands red the stubble yellow
What I used to love I now use least

Wooden crutch this is winter
The warriors make merry indoors
Nobody visits my little room

Except you my mute my familiar
Stand by my unsteady tongue
Wiser a straight wand than a crooked talker

Stay by my side sustain me
Bear with me wooden brother
I am bereaved. Be hard with me.
Unmoved. Ignore my chatter.

Old Age is having its fun
My hair and my teeth are hidden
And you can't tell me where to find them
I envy you your erect stem
Could still impress the young

I say that swine Old Age
Has hidden my teeth and my hair
I'll keep you close to me
Women like your stem better than mine.

The wind cracks. There are white skirts
To the trees. A stag is brave. The hill bare.
I am frail. My steps very slow.

A leaf like this pushed about by the breeze.
I'll be sorry for it. Fate they call it.
Already old. Born this year.

All I craved for in those days I now refuse.
A young woman. A hard foe. An unbroken stallion.
Somehow they no longer suit me.

I have four servers left. I can name them.
They never fail. Infection.
Cough. Thorned Ague. Chill Old Age.

I am old. Alone. Ugly with cold
I once lay in a royal bed
Now I am unwarmed. Wretched.

The shape of a crook. A broken fool.
Fickle. Savage. Uncivil.
Even those left who loved me avoid me

And no girl comes by. Who would want to see me?
Not even Death
I can't go out to call him in

Or call my sons back from the grave
Gwawr and Gwên! I can't sleep thinking about them!

The night I was born
It all began
My long life is a proverb about pain.

Adapted from 'Canu Llywarch Hen'.

Sweet Research

Research is more important
Than tinkering with verse
How can you count the pieces
While picking at the Purse?
I'll give up angling for Inspiration
And fish back-numbers of *The Nation*.

What is this that rises
Like wine to my weak head
Discovery of discoveries
J.G.G. died in bed!
He married well. A Yorkshire dame
We must find out her maiden name . . .

Please understand my chagrin
The palm's snatched from my fist
I find it's all been printed in
The *Illinois State Bulletin*
Ah well . . . so what. There's music yet
To wring out of the old *North Wales Gazette*.

Now here's a Revelation!
A big mistake's been made
P.H. was born in Bangor
And not in Biggleswade.
He died of drink. And bankrupt too
But not in 1792.

What profit for a mortal
To try and light his lamp
On the bright side of Parnassus
With matches that are damp?
On sweet Research I'll live content
And let the college pay the rent

I'll beaver through these papers
Like a weevil in the wood
Establish beyond question
What's little understood:
January 14 *was* the date
But not in 1788.

And I shall make quite certain
Before I take the field
That no one else has published
Obliging me to yield
In appendix or revised edition
That note of grudging recognition.

What joy to sweat *Mutatis*
Mutandis to research
In the salt mines of the Stack Room
Till the prof drops off his perch:
To find, O academic bliss,
All previous work was wrong on this.

So be it. When I'm crossing
The chilly river Styx
I shall hear a distant trumpet
Blow like an asterisk
As I leave for posthumous publication
My footnotes to a grateful nation.

Adapted from R.Williams Parry's 'Chwilota'.

J.S.L.

A bright bird lighted in the sheltered yard
Out of another sky and all his colours dazzled
Our native poultry. Above his head
There was consternation in the dovecote, the kind of fuss
You find among the well-fed and the tame.
The bright bird was unwise. He sang his own song
Unaccompanied, on a new scale
Without sympathy or support. Not so much wrong
As solitary. He was bound to fail.
That's you, my rejected friend. You were a fool.
As for us, sound men of learning, we serve tea
While you serve time. The afternoon is on our side
Nothing disturbs our classic calm, no parish pump
Concerns. No echoing sighs. No prison cells.
We munch with precision our trimmed and buttered toast
You sew your mail-bags for the General Post.

*Adapted from R.Williams Parry's tribute to Saunders Lewis when he was
imprisoned in 1937 and dismissed from his university post.*

Before the Deluge

The tramway climbs from Merthyr to Dowlais
The slime of a snail on the mound of slag
This was once Cymru, now a dump
With cinemas derelict and rain on the barren tips.
The pawnbrokers have shut up shop: the labour exchange
Rules this dead land:
The face of the earth crawls with the last corruption:

My life is likewise, seconder to those motions
That move from committee to committee
To jack the old country back on its creaking feet:
Better maybe to stand on the corner in Tonypandy
Looking up the valley and down the valley
At a scattered wreck sinking in the mud of despair.
Stand like a tip, men and rubble equally discarded.

We are already dead and our eyes are dust
We sucked the drugged waters of death in our mother's milk
We cannot bleed as our forefathers bled
Or work with hands that have grown without thumbs:
When our feet are crushed in a fall
That makes it easier to bow in the free clinic
Raise a cap with respect to a wooden leg the insurance and
        Sir Alfred Mond's pension:
We are tamed. We no longer nurse a proud language or any
                        resentment
And our gift to the world is a row of Labour MPs.

Adapted from the opening of Saunders Lewis's 'Y Dilyw 1939'.

St Michael's Little Summer 1941

Spring came and went with little sunlight
To pick out the blue flash of the swallow under the bridge;
Nursed by the warm wet summer
Green shoots sprouted in the August corn:
With the mail so slow from Egypt, from Singapore
Women held their ears closer to a voice in a box . . .
A terrible slaughter in Russia I should think . . .
And the rain dripped like worry day after day
On backs bent with that eloquence beyond words:
That was the war in our village,
An assembly in the distance, a wall of doom approaching,
A black threat hiding the lightning;
And on the mantlepiece the English voice in the box
Our tiny share of mass communication
Announcing and pronouncing
While the postman mutters his own news from door to door
With names that are nearer, Cardiff . . . Swansea . . . Our South,
Retailing unspecified fear; faces, tongues are strangers;

Who can think, who can speak his mind
Except that confident voice in the box boasting
Our navy, *our* airforce, and we more hesitant than ever
To believe that we are we
As we move like people under a spell
From the yard to the field
Where our hands may feel things solid as old certainties
And other centuries
In the August rain.

But the wind turned. The early morning mist
Was scattered by the slow power of a royal sun.
There was a breadth of afternoon and a sunset of streaming
                                                    banners
Before the Great Bear closed his arms around the night sky;

There was a loading of carts in the cornfield
And in the orchard the dew glittered
On the still gossamer that hung between green apples;
This was Michael's gift, a hill to restore us,

A sanctuary of summer haze in late September
Balm before winter, before the testing time, before the dark
Before weighing anchor and sailing like Ulysses
Beyond the last headland of the living:
'O Brothers, do not avoid the brief vigil
The last experience, what remains for us to learn
Of the splendour and misery of this world . . .'
And Dante saw him with Diomede, two in one fire.

Michael, lover of mountains pray in our hills.
Michael, friend of the maimed and the sick, bear with us.

Adapted from Saunders Lewis's 'Haf Bach Mihangel 1941'.

Dartmoor 1917

Bars burn again across your eyes. Doors
Clang upon your ears
Lags, lunatics, sow and reap their sighs
Break acres of remorse on those cold moors.

August you saw spread heavy sunsets
Like slaughter, blood into pools and ditches.
November came distributing mists
Imprisoning the prison. The nights belonged to witches.

You heard them. The congregation of the damned
Assembled and in session with their dogs
Their screech owls and their endless cries
Of pain and guilt. Shapes writhing in the fog:

But in your cell you gripped your necklace of goodness, your lucky
                                                              charm,
The blue river Tywi winding between farm and farm.

Adapted from Gwenallt's 'Dartmoor'.

What is a Man?

What is living? Finding a great hall
Inside a cell.
What is knowing? One root
To all the branches.

What is believing? Holding out
Until relief comes.
And forgiving? Crawling through thorns
To the side of an old foe.

What is singing? Winning back
The first breath of creation:
And work should be a song
Made of wheat or wood.

What is statecraft? Something
Still on all fours.
And defence of the realm?
A sword thrust in a baby's hand.

What is being a nation? A talent
Springing in the heart.
And love of country? Keeping house
Among a cloud of witness.

What is this world to the great powers?
A circle turning.
And to the lowly of the earth?
A cradle rocking.

Adapted from Waldo Williams's 'Pa Beth yw Dyn?'

Plagiarising Parry-Williams

Care about Wales? Well, I do and I don't.
The committed spring their own trap. I certainly won't.

One just happens to live here. It's a nice enough place
Not a boil on the back of beyond. As for the race

If one dare make use of such an imprecise word,
Self absorbed no doubt and hypocritical too. But in this world

Who isn't? Admittedly one can have too much melodious moaning
It's important to distinguish between whingeing, wailing and
                                                        groaning

And maybe the constant twitter of nervously nationalist noises
Distracts our subsidised bards from promoting worthier causes

But at least the sounds are local. Not media manufactured
The smaller facts of life are less easily fractured

So I'll make for the hills! Avoid all sententious chatter
Get back to where I was born. The mountain and things that
                                                        matter

Here I stand. Not exactly Luther but relieved to get away.
Not a flag in sight. Or a hoarding. Just the light of common day.

There's the first peak I clambered: all the rugged truth of the land
There's the lake, and the stream, and the crag: and right at hand

My father's house. Where else between heaven and earth
Can I recapture the sound of the folk who gave me birth?

Why am I shaking? Where's that scientific resolve
That keeps sentiment at bay? Homeland. Heimat. Bro.

These are claws of Cymreictod clutching at my breast
Harsh signals to respond. Can I avoid the Test?

Adapted from T. H. Parry-Williams's 'Hon'.

Ar Adeg o Derfysg

Hon
Ar adeg o derfysg yn cychwyn ar ei thaith
Fel cenedl gyfan yn cerdded yn ei chwsg
Heb docyn heb ddogfen heb gyfeiriad
Heb bacio'n iawn ac yn llusgo hen gelfi
Ei thynged mewn falis hen ffasiwn drom
A chysgod o'r enw Arthur yn ei hebrwng
Er mwyn ei chlywed hi'n sisial tiwn gron ei glod
Dathlu fel hysbyseb gylchol ei enwogrwydd
Amherthnasol: wedi blino gormod i fathu
Geiriau newydd heb sôn am drwshio'r hen enwau
Sy'n disgyn fel daint crib bregus o'r hen fag
Lledr heb ei gau'n iawn hyd y pafin gwlyb.
Heb grib heb offeryn danheddog sut fedr
Morwyn ddilychwin ddichlynaidd ac yn y blaen
Gadw trefn ar ei gwallt?

Dirdynnir yr arwr gan ei awydd i'w chynorthwyo.
Mewn ffaith neu mewn llyfr hanes peth hyll
Yw cofnod o ferch, hen neu ifanc, hyll neu hardd,
Yn marw'n gelain ddienw ar ochr y lôn
Ond ysywaeth nid oes gan gysgod fysedd.

Dim ond atgof o wahoddiadau i ben y daith
Ac amlinelliad o ganiatâd cynllunio
Tŷ di-dreth-ar-werth di-dreth-y-pen di-enw
Ar stad un o faesdrefi mwyaf dewisol Annwn
Yn dygyfor ag atgofion a'r muriau'n wlyb
Dan wlith yr addewidion

Y dodrefn heb gyrraedd ond lle i eistedd
Ar set gyfan o'r Gwyddoniadur a'r Ford Gron.
Rhwng cadwyn o farfau Rhita Gawr
Modrwy Llew Llwyfo a charnau merlod Thomas Gee
Ymestyn grisiau gwydr i'r seithfed llawr
Ond, meddai Arthur, gan fod grisial yn fregus
Cystal symud am i lawr.

137

Yna mae'r ogofeydd enwog, yn groes i'r disgwyl,
Wedi eu dodrefnu'n foethus
Fel llwyfan o dan lifolau. Ac yna mae'r gorffennol i gyd ar gael
Ar fideo lliw Pal-secam-is-deitlau
At eich gwasanaeth – yn ailadrodd
Camgymeriadau mwyaf lliwgar yr hil
Ac o'r blychau sain llais y Llew ei hun
Yn rhuo o'r llwyfan ac yn cuddio
Yn ei flwch baco arian gedor y gantores
Sydd hefyd am roi tro ar yr anthem ddagreuol . . .
'Hyfrydwch hanes yw'r cariad sy'n cydio
Er na wêl
Yr ymadawedig
Y blodau sy'n gwywo ar ei bedd.'

Cardiau Post

'Flys troi 'nghefn ar y cwbl
Cecru cyfryngau gwg y gyfraith
Edliw gwleidyddion hunandybus o graff
Aflwyddiant gwlad a chymdeithas
Cofio mwy nag wythnos ar y tro.
Ydi'r llun hwn wrth dy fodd?

Mae'r llanw'n cyrraedd i'r un llinell
Yma buost yn sefyll fel duwies addfwyn o'r heli
A'r un hen wylanod yn ymestyn
Edau sidan amser rhwng tir a nef
Wrth alw ar dy ôl.
'Does dim o'i le ar atgofion sy'n rhoi hwb i'r galon.
Mawr oedd ein braint a'r llanw'n llyfu'n wasaidd
Bysedd traed ein plant.

ii

'Does fawr o ddiben mewn cyfarch neb
Mwy na siarad fel lli'r afon wrthot ti dy hun.
Be sy gen i i ddweud wrth hen farchfilwr
A'r Fi Si ar ei frest ond anadl eiddigeddus edmygedd
Neu'r wraig gyfoethog a'i chŵn, y cyn-arwr pêl-droed,
Y newyddiadurwr ar ei wyliau? Gallaf gynnig
Gwydriad i bob un wrth reswm a chanu
'Iechyd da' ond beth wedyn? Cofleidio
Estron ferch ac ymddiheuro am y camgymeriad?
Cyfeillach od heb fod gennych iaith gyffredin
Ond odiach fyth rhannu iaith heb fod gennych ddim i'w ddweud.
Diolch bod nos yn disgyn
Rhwng dau ddydd a'r tocyn adref
Yn cysgu o dan fy nghesail.

iii

Didostur wyliau. Cymanfa cŵn yr ardal
Gwynt y sierra'n gyrru iasau diflas
Ar draws y gwres. Beth yw cryfder perthyn?
Fy nghhortynnau sy wedi ymestyn yn rhy bell
A dim ond grym dur y gwagle, deddf disgyrchiant

Yn dal y byw a'r meirw y pîn a'r cychod a'r rheilffyrdd
At ei gilydd. Ym mhrisma dyddiau segur
Ymddengys mai dim ond dy absenoldeb di
Sy'n dal pen rheswm ynghyd. Yma
Gwelaf ddiarfogi daioni byw gan lu y gwyll
A'r dail crin wrth fy nhraed fel llygaid
Eneidiau coll.

iv

Faint gwell hedfan bant
Mewn byd sy'n crebachu? Taflu dy hun
Fel penfras neu benbwl o bwll i bwll
Glanio ar dir sych yng ngolau'r lleuad
A gweld dy hun ar dy waetha
Ym murddrych anfaddeugar bar porth awyr arall?

Ceisia efelychu môr-gudyn a'th deimlyddion
Yn bodio creigiau crugyll fel dyn dall yn chwilio am gynefin
Ac aros nes dysgu wrth deimlo
Mai ti dy hun yw'r graig sy'n barod i ddisgwyl
O leia am filenium arall am
Ymweliad yr ysbryd.

Cyflwr Dŵr

Ydi dŵr yn ymboeni beunydd am ei gyflwr gwlyb?
Bwriwch fod ganddo enaid hylif a llygaid
Yn llawn dagrau'n methu gwahaniaethu rhwng dechrau a diwedd.
Dyhead yw'r llyfeirio am offeryn
Tebyg i gyllell amser sy'n tymheru cymeriad
Ac yn naddu cnawd: sy'n crino gwefusau
Ac yn dysgu dail coed i ddisgyn fel ebyrth milwrol:
Chwilio am elfen i ddofi'r diderfyn symud
Mewn ymdrech olaf cofleidio a nid boddi'r gwir.

Hanes Plwyfol

i

Yr eglwys 'slawer dydd oedd y fan a'r lle
I brofi digyfnewidra pethau:
Y cerrig nadd yn cynnal y canrifoedd
Fel goslef y Rheithor yn cyfarch
Ei annwyl gariadus frodyr – a fawr neb
Ond chwiorydd yn gwrando – fel pe bai
Sidanydd yn dal i deyrnasu. Anwybydder
Sŵn dŵr yn berwi yn y pibau rhydlyd
A gwrando'n fwy astud ar wich
Dolefus organ fyr o wynt.

ii

Ble bynnag yr ei di, meddai gwraig y gweinidog
Cofio gofyn i bawb sut hwyl sydd arnynt, ond cofio
Hefyd peidio mynd ar eu gofyn. A pheidio byth
Â brolio dy hun na hyd yn oed cyraeddiadau
Dy dylwyth. Gad hynny i'r Saeson.
Ni fydd ar y rhan fwyaf o drigolion y dinasoedd
Eisiau dy weld heb sôn am dy glywed.
Mae si bod y Dalai Llama dan wenu wedi cau
Ei ddrws yng ngwyneb gohebydd teledu enwog.

iii

Sut y gwyddost ti fod Duw yn caru gwas anfoddog?
Am fod yr Hen Air yn drwch ohonynt.
A'r adeg hynny hefyd yn cyfeiliorni
Yn amlach na pheidio. Serch hynny,
Frodyr a chwiorydd, parhawn i barchu
Eu hawdurdod gan fod eu harthio'n
Gwreiddio ym mhridd ein hamheuon brau.

iv

Mae gen i radd Rhydychen, meddai'r Person
Ond be sydd yn erbyn bod yn syml a chlir?

Os yw daioni yn anodd i'w ddeall
Pwy ohonom fydd fyth gadwedig?

Nid arholiad ydyw iechydwriaeth
Ond rhad ras rhatach na'r papur-am-ddim.

Ar y llaw arall cofier
Bod cloch ym mhen rhaffau'r addewidion
Nad yw'n canu yn y dafarn
Ar ôl deg o'r gloch.

Cofiwch hyn hefyd.
Os yw'r gwir yn syml
Mae celwydd yn symlach fyth
Ac yn gymaint haws i'w lyncu.

v

Arglwydd Dduw nid dyma'r bobl
Y bûm yn dyheu eu gwasanaethu
Na syllu ar eu hwynebau dyrchafedig . . .

Ta waeth am hynny, was,
Darostwng y diawliaid
Fel rhannau anystywallt
O dy gorff dy hun: ac nac anghofia
Gadw'r gist yn y festri
Yn llawn o sachau lliain a lludw.

vi

Pwy sydd ar ôl i brofi bod hyn oll yn wir?
Byddwch yn barod, bensiynwyr,
I deimlo'n euog. Waeth pa mor foethus
Cerbydau'r cwmni teithio, maes parcio
Saif lle safai Horeb gynt a'r eglwys a'r festri
Ym meddiant perchennog sioe ceffylau bach.

Cara Signora

Eisteddai o flaen y drws
A'i dwylo fel torch yn gwywo yn ei chôl,
Holi ac ateb ei hun. Nid cyffes ond her.
Ein swydd ni, ymwelwyr a basgedi ar ein breichiau
Oedd sefyll yn y gwres a gwrando ei chŵyn.

'Be fedra-i wneud a honna isio fy lladd?
'Dw inna hefyd yn sylwedd byw, nid aderyn mud.'

Llygad hon
Oedd y pin dur yn cadw'r cyfan yn ei le.
Crebachai ymylon yr olygfa fel cerdyn post
Yn crino yn yr haul. Crafai'r ieir o dan yr olewydd.
Gweithiai Luigi, ei hunig fab, yn y winllan.
Stelciai Camilla, y ferch-yng-nghyfraith, yn y llofft
Yn moeli'i chlust wrth berarogli ei chesail.

'Rheibes! Mae hi am fy lladd.
A mi laddith yntau wedyn, unwaith
Y bydda inna allan o'r ffordd . . .
O na faswn i'n medru ymosod arni
Gyda phicell yn lle geiria, yr hwran ddiymwared.'

Delw ddu ar fainc yn traddodi dedfryd
Camilla, druan. Welsoch chi neb erioed mor annhebyg i hwran:
Athrawes plant bach, fel y bu, a'i llais yn aros
Mor felys foethus forwynol ag erioed.
A'i hunig wendid, yn ôl ei chyfaddefiad swil,
Siocoled a phethau melys.

'Fi ddaru orfodi'r oen llywaeth i'w phriodi
Er mwyn cael etifedd ac er mwyn
Gwneud dyn ohono yn lle lob maldodus.
Wnâi o run swydd drwy'r dydd ond
Tynnu llunia. Adfeilion ac ati
Oedd 'i betha fo. Hen eglwysi a phlastai
A gora oll os oedd 'u penna ar fynd iddyn.

Methu pob arholiad neu ohirio eistedd
Trwy gymryd arno fod yn sâl. Creadur felly oedd o
Yn dyheu am fod yn rhywun gwell na'i gilydd
Heb y drafferth o ennill y cymwystera . . .
A minna'n ddigon gwirion i'w amddiffyn
Rhag cyfiawn lid fy ngŵr. A dyma'r wobr.
Eistedd fel hen gath yn yr haul
Yn colli blew ac ymladd am ei gwynt.
I be mae diarhebion yn dda?'

Safem heb fedru symud, gwahoddedigion
Ar eu ffordd i yfed gwin melys a theisennau bach
Yng nghwmni'r Gamilla hon
Cyn mynd i hel ffigys a chnau ym mherllan
Luigi ei gŵr. 'Pwy oedd piau be?'
Gofynnai dŵr y llyn wrth wenu ar yr haul.

'Un felly oedd o, fy mab, nes priodi hon.
Dim gwaith yn 'i groen o. Ond yn awr
Mae o wrthi o fore gwyn tan nos.
Yn gyhyra i gyd, dyn yn ei fan
Wedi gwirioni ar wraig dew amhlantadwy.
Maen nhw'n gwagio 'nhŷ i ac yn gwerthu
'Mhetha a neb yn codi llaw i'w rhwystro.
At bwy medra-i droi? Y *questura*? Y *carabinieri*?
"Does dim ymyrryd i fod," meddai'r *Sindaco*
"Mewn helyntion teuluol." (A minnau'n gwybod
Fod y cythraul hyll – a'i dad o'i flaen o –
Yn curo'i blant ac yn cicio'i wraig.)
Gwagio 'nhŷ i ddarn wrth ddarn.
Faint o barch sydd gan yr hanner byw
I'r hanner marw?'

Dim chwa o wynt. Crogai'r *bandiera rossa*'n
Hy ond yn llipa fel llawes wleidyddol wag o dŵr
Y castell Monaldeschi. Disgwyliai
Wrth bawb i gyfarch gwell iddi wrth gerdded heibio
Gan gynnwys yr hen bendefig ar ei ffordd
I'r offeren. Sul, gŵyl a gwaith cusanai hwnnw
Ei llaw dde a'i galw yn '*cara signora*'.

'Mefl ar bob merch-yng-nghyfraith. Mae gan hon
Fam fursennaidd yn byw mewn twlc
Yn Viterbo. Nid cynt fy nghladdu
Na fydd honno yn cysgu yn fy ngwely plu,
Eistedd yn fanma, debyg, a'r pendefig
Ar ei ffordd i'r offeren yn cusanu'i llaw –
Tydi'r hen greadur ddim yn gweld yn dda –
A'i galw yn "*cara signora*" . . . Chwitha,
Ymwelwyr gwybodus o wlad arall, dwedwch
Ai fel'ma mae hi dros wyneb daear lawr?'

Eistedd o flaen y drws fel delw ddu,
Carcharor ym mharadwys. Sawl cerdyn post
Sydd ei eisiau i guddio briwiau Bod? I ni
Doedd dim dewis ond ei chusanu ar ddwy foch wywedig
Cyn troi i mewn i'r tŷ.

Carchar Gweir

Carchardai. Amlosgfeydd. Coedwigoedd gwag.
Ceidwadaeth penglog. Llysnafedd atgof
Ar y muriau gwyn.
Penyd carchar cadwyno cyfarwydd
Nid dileu cof.

Cysur cofio cariad yn nos wen carchar.
Ar y buarth at wasanaeth y swyddogion
Golau euraidd y llusern
Fel atgof ohonot

Llygaid unllygeidiog gwyliwr ym mogail y drws
Dyrnod dyled troed a throsol, ond hefyd
Atsain malu esgyrn, mwg cnawd yn llosgi,
Gwaedd poenydio, seiniau gwae
Na feddwai fyth y synnwyr
O waelod cantre diwaelod.

Braf oedd chwarae broch yng nghod
Nes i yrdd drws y llys gau am fy ngwddf . . .
'Taw hyd y mynni fusgrell ŵr
Hyd at flwyddyn i heno neu ddiwedd canrif
Cei blethu pwyll a phryder
A'r sŵn yn dy ben a glywi ac yn y cynteddau
Fydd esgyrn yn cracio fel cnau mewn gefail.
Cei glywed cyrff cenedlaethau yn digoni
Ar y cigweiniau a'r awel yn drewi
Pydredd a llosgi.'

Y sibrwd ym mreuddwyd carcharor
A'r sôn am achub yw cynnig llofnod a gwadu
O oes i oes sylfeini cyfeillgarwch a ffydd.
Os dal penrheswm gyda'r awdurdodau
Os oes gobaith eistedd eto wrth fwrdd cyfeddach
Ac ysgwyd llaw â threfnyddion y wledd
A chymysgu â'r gwŷr a'r gwragedd gorau
Rhaid bod yn barod i fwyta darnau amheuthun o'n gilydd.
Ysglyfaeth yw fy nghymydog, saig
Newydd a'i enw'n addurno'r pâté ar y meniw.

147

Yn y cyfamser taith igam-ogam gwyfyn
Hediad gwamal a ddaw i ben fel pylor
Rhwng gwadn esgid a cherrig oer amlosgfa
Ac yn y celloedd arwyr anarwrol
Heb gyfle creu yn disgwyl eu tro
Carchar cyffion caethiwed

O flodau haf heb olau dydd
Tu mewn i'r barrau haearn hyn
Derbyn fel gorchudd we pry cop y canrifoedd
Ceisia ystofi enfysoedd ar draws yr edau
Yn lle cenhedlu etifedd. Ble erbyn hyn
Mewn byd ac amser y saif llys haf Hyfaidd Hen?

Smaldod llywodraeth nid echelydd chwil
Yw peidio â datgelu ai ar neu wrth
Y bwrdd y byddaf yn y wledd derfynol.
Ystyr unigrwydd yw sefyll a syrthio
Yn yr agen fain lle gall oes o brofiad lechu
Lle na bydd llawn dy god di fyth.

Mae pawb yn gwybod y deil pregethwr di-gynghanedd
Mai dyn sy'n llywodraethu a dyn sy'n berig.
Arnat ti mae'r bai fod Duw wedi pwdu
Mae gennyt enaid annelwig
Galw am y gair petryal i ddal dy bentwr o lwch.

Y meddwl yn arafu, croen yn cleisio
Erys helaethrwydd ambell freuddwyd
O ganol gwely peiswyn y mae Rhyddid Bod
Fel blodyn unig, llygaid undydd
Ar ganol diffeithwch yr oes oesoedd
Anorffenedig yw meddwl amdanat
Nes at y tragwyddol na grym y pla

Yn nos y carchar atgof ohonot
Yn goleuo darnau gwydr y meddwl

Pwyll yn wynebu pryder dros
Ddibyn y dudalen olaf
Yn y ffwrn yn y pentwr o lwch
Ar wahân i fymryn o gariad
Be fydd ar ôl?

Norchia

Diwrnod i'r brenin yn Norchia
Pa frenin? Tarcwiniws. Neb llai.
Gelyn y Rhufeiniaid rhwth a chocyn hitio
Cenedlaethau athrawon Lladin
Yn tin-droi yn eu cylch llwch sialc.

O barch i Darcwin ymddygwn megis pererinion
A'n lluniaeth a'n llawenydd ar ein cefnau
Malwod canol oed heb arf na dryll
Ar wahân i'm ffon amrwd taro'r prysg
I roi gwybod i'r gwiberod swrth ein bod ni wrth law.

Treiddio'r *burrone,* croesi'r cerrig rhyd,
Tramwy rhigolau creigiog y ffrydlifau
A diolch am byncio'r adar, edrych
I'r wybren a gweld holl gorau cymysg
Dail y coed a'u cegau ar agor
O dan arweiniad haul gordyfiant
A'u cân werdd yn cuddio llwybrau a beddrodau.

'Y ni sydd ar goll,' meddet tithau. Chlywais i
Erioed sôn fod beddrodau'n symud.
Wrth gwrs, fe fu lladron y canrifoedd yn malu
Sarcoffagi yn eu rhaib am drysor
A brawd Napoleon Fawr yn eu mysg
Yn rhodresa diffyg parch arferol
Y traddodiad ymerodrol. Mussolini'r un sut.
Rhufeinwyr wrth eu hewyllys. Gwylliaid
Yn ysu am arwisgo anrhaith mewn aur a phorffor.
Os yw'r goleuni yn datgan celwydd
Ai'r tywyllwch yn unig sy'n dweud y gwir?

'Cymaint o dyfiant,' meddwn innau. 'Be
Sy'n tyfu mewn beddrod, deuda?'
'Rhagor o dywyllwch,' meddet tithau.
A'th grechwen yn dychryn yr adar
A'r gwiberod fel ei gilydd.

Brwydro ymlaen am awr, crafangio,
Cymynu drain a mieri, crafu a chraffu
Nes gweld rhyfeddod prin: dyn penfelyn
Mewn cot wen laes yn sefyll â'i gefn at ddrws
Hanner ffordd i fyny clogwyn. Ai angel
Neu archoffeiriad wrth geg ogof brenin braw?
Y tresel o'i flaen yn allor a'i draed yn uwch
Na chryndod dail brigau'r aethnen, a'r cŷn
Yn ei law fel yr ellyn a fu ddwy fil a hanner
Blwyddyn yn ôl yn llaw Atws y dewin.
A holltodd y garreg hogi ym meddwl y teyrn.

O barch i'r chwedl eisteddasom
Fel tystion mud mor ostyngedig
Â gwin a chaws y fro.

Yng ngŵydd brenhiniaeth y beddrod
Un oedd yr hynafiaethydd ifanc a'r brudiwr hen
A'n presenoldeb dof yn wrogaeth o ryw fath
I rym oesoesol Etrwria'r byw a'r meirw

Nes i sŵn aflafar rwygo'r awyr denau.
Milwyr gorfodol yr Eidal ar ymarfer NATO
Wedi cael cip ar ferched ar ben yr allt gyferbyn
Ac yn tanio eu harfau fel ergydion ffalig
A bygwth canu.

'Disgynyddion y lladron,' meddet tithau,
'Yn dal i halogi athrylith esmwyth y lle,'
Ond yn aflonyddu dim ar yr hynafiaethydd ifanc
Yn dirwyn ei wyddoniaeth rhwng ei fysedd
Fel Atws ers talwm yn barod i roi'r byd
A'r brenin yn ei le.

*Norchia: Dyffryn beddrodau Etrwscaidd yn Lazio, rhyw hanner can
milltir i'r gogledd o Rufain.*

Aralleirio Montale*

Aros am dipyn, wleidydd,
Nes bydd y newyddion wedi chwyddo'n hanes
Pryd hynny a dim cynt
Bydd hynt y gwybedyn
Yn ehediad eryr,
Gwich ystlum
Yn atsain Dies Irae.

Y ffaith yw bod y byd
Yn berwi efo graddedigion
Oni ddylid eu gwarchod
Mewn tyllau nes daw pethau'n well?
Gorwedd y dyfodol
Er gwell medd ein gwleidyddion –
Neu er gwaeth meddent ar dro –
Mewn rhewgell a Duw a ŵyr
Sut mae eu datmar
Yn yr hinsawdd sydd ohoni.

Pob parch i sgrech yr ystlum.
Pa fiwsig sy'n gweddu'n well
Ar gyfer yr hir nosi?
Pentwr du toddedig
Yw batri ein gwareiddiad
Ac ni wyddom
Er lles pwy

Da oedd gwneud dyn
Ar ei ddelw ei hun
Ond ai doeth
Llenwi'r ddaear â delwau?
Gwaddod yw'r gwirionedd
I borthi gwyfyn a llygod bach.

*Eugenio Montale (1896–1981).

152

Montale, Fwy neu Lai

Beunydd bodio darnau digyswllt
Sy'n bygwth ystyr
Ond byth yn cyrraedd cyfanswm
A dywed y llwfr sy'n llechu ynof
Diolch am hynny.

Pe bai amser gennyf a chof digoll
Gosodaswn bob iot o brofiatach yn ei le
A chodi cyfrif cywir
Twr o ffigyrau, colofn
Rhifolion nefol yn cyrraedd at y sêr
Boed rheini'n rhewi neu beidio.

Ofer yw'r cais
Ac eto unig siawns ystyr
Yw ymarfer â chysondeb.

Dal ati, was
Er mor anwadal yr elfennau
Yr eiliad sy'n difa,
Y pridd sy'n gwrthod anadlu
Y dŵr anghyfiaith sy'n llosgi yn lle tân

Codwn ddinasoedd mwg ar draws yr awyr

Dim ond yn y diwedd darganfod
Mai'r dwyfol yn unig sy'n cydio
Llyfu a llyncu ynghyd
Rhwng y blys a'r blas
Llond llwy o farwolaeth
Yw'r cyfanswm.

Poughkeepsie*

Ffaith i'w hanwesu?
Daeth ei hen hen daid o Gymru –
Mae pawb yn dod o rywle –
A rhywdro cyn cychwyn neu ar ôl cyrraedd
Mi dorrodd ei enw mewn ysgrifen amrwd
Ar wynebddalen y Beibl hwn,
Haciau hy o dan lythrennau coch
Enw parchus Peter Williams:
Cymaint â hynny mae 'i or-or-ŵyr
O Boughkeepsie yn medru ei ddeall.

Gofynnodd yn wylaidd faint oedd gwerth
Mil cant naw deg a dau o dudalennau
Na fedrai mo'u darllen
Gan fod pris ar bopeth yn y wlad honno
Ond dŵr a rhyddid cyfansoddiadol
Hyd yn oed hen gyfrol drwsgwl
Yn hel llwch yn y llofft afalau.

'Gwerth y byd,' meddwn wrtho,
Y creadur siriol a'i wyneb a'i fol
Yn sgleinio gan lawnder ac anwybod pêr,
A chywilyddio wedyn wrth gofio
Am wraig prifathro prifysgol yng Nghymru bell
Yn cynnig pentwr o hen Feiblau Cymraeg i artist arbrofol
Ar gyfer eu darnio a'u chwistrellu
Gyda lliwiau a glud ar ôl eu hanner llosgi . . .
A minnau'n sôn dim am werth.

'Roedd y gor-or-ŵyr yn barotach i dderbyn fy ngair
Na mi fy hun. Be di gwerth
Clogwyn Du'r Arddu, crawc cigfran,
Pell ffenestri'n cochi, y pellter
Rhwng y warthol a'r llwch
A'r eiliad unigryw pan gafodd Williams
A'r hen-hen-daid eu hachub?

Ein baich ni yw hel y profion
Nid y cyfrwng yw'r neges neu buasai'r ddaear hon
Yn olosg erbyn hyn.
Sut mae hel profion a'r gweithredoedd nerthol
I gyd yn perthyn i'r gelyn?
Tybed oes modd eu dosbarthu
Fel hysbysebion sebon ar ti-fi?

Gwylwyr y bumed frenhiniaeth
Y mae darn o ystyr Bod fel darn o Gymru
Yn hel llwch fel cyfrinach ym Mhoughkeepsie draw.

*Enw tref yn nhalaith Efrog Newydd y mae'r Americanwyr yn tueddu i
ddweud yn ysmala amdano. Ystyr yr enw, medd y cyhoeddiad cwbl
Americanaidd hwnnw, yr Encyclopaedia Britannica yw 'y llety-to-
brwyn-yn-ymyl-y-ffynnon-fach' (adlais bellennig ond digamsyniol Eingl-
Sacsonaidd o gyfieithu twristaidd yr ydym mor gyfarwydd ag ef yn
Llanfairpwllgwyngyll).

Cymodi â Ffawd

Yn bump ar hugain oed cyrraedd Milan
A'r rhyfel ar ben, y rhyfel hwn o leiaf,
Corff tarw unben olaf y penynys
A chorff ei ordderch yn crogi yn y gwres
Eu pennau am i lawr fel bustych yn disgwyl eu blingo
Ebrill a fling.

Y lladd drosodd am dro ac eto ansicrwydd oedd y cwbl.
Beth yw pris cydwybod? Beddau dros dro ar y maes.
Beth am ein hawydd awchus i oroesi
Wrth edrych ar olion y frwydr yn y mynyddoedd
Fel tristwch oesol, y tanciau a'r bidogau eisoes yn rhydu
O gwmpas y beddau bas? Pen pwy yn y sach?
Fawr o le i farwnadau ymysg cymaint o gyrff
Dim ond sŵn y pryfed fel pryder yn yr haul.

Tybed ai grym ewyllys oedd gwaith cydwybod
Pam marw'r rhain a minnau'n dal i fyw?
Gofynnod yw'r Presennol, eiliad anfeidrol
Y pabi coch unigol. Nid diwedd y rhyfel
Yw diwedd y daith

Ond dechrau taith arall. Ac nid ymchwil
Am ffordd ymwared na hyd yn oed be wna i nesa
Na sut i gyfiawnhau parhau bod fy mod.
Anesmwythyd mwy cyffrous na hynny. Bloedd

Ar ganol pryd o fwyd yng nghegin yr ysbyty.
Dychwel y gallu i ryfeddu. O'r marmor gwyn
Y glanweithdra a phertrwydd syber merched y Croce Rossa.
Symud ymlaen i'r ffin, tu draw i Como
Gweld plant ysgol yn neidio i'r llyn i ddathlu heddwch
Moduro'r *jeep* heibio i Dongo
Lle daliwyd y tarw unben a'i drysor.

Cyrraedd troed yr Alpau a'r rheini'n sefyll o'n blaen
Fel terfyn bod. Y lle i droi yn ôl. Droedfeddi'n is
Na chell y meudwy. Camarweiniol pob trosiad.
Os yw popeth yn debyg i rywbeth arall
Y mae pob cyffelybiaeth yn ffordd ymwared ffug.

Yn bump ar hugain oed
Nid oes un frawddeg a saif fel craig gwirionedd
Na bloedd na chychwynnai afalans mewn lle fel hwn

Tybed oes rhaid rhyfela wedi'r cwbl
Yng nglyn cysgod angau arall, codi cleddyf chwedl?

Derbyn y ffawd Arthuraidd. Ar y llyn
Daeth cysgod cwch yn nes i'r lan ac arno
Dywysoges ifanc. 'Tyrd ataf a dymchwel furiau hunan.
Dyma bris cydwybod. Gafael yn fy llaw.'

Ar y Guincho

Mewn restaurant ar lan y môr
Gwelais gimychiaid cyhyrog yn bwyta pobl
Canmolasant leiniau can y byrddau
A rhyfeddasant at lesni'r môr yn yr haul
A mydr mingam y tonnau mân.

Hael eu geiriau hefyd am y cig coch a gwyn
A hwylustod y dull o'u cadw'n fyw mewn cewyll
Rhwng y creigiau a'r llanw
Cyn y berwi a'r darnio.

Gwin hen gyfeillgarwch oedd nodd y gyfeillach
A ffynhonnell darfelydd a rhyfeddu
'Beth pe baem ninnau'n saig rhwng y dail gwyrdd
A'r boblach yn cadrilio o'n cwmpas
Mewn dillad llaes i glindarddach eu hofferynnau cerdd?

Diolch fod gennym fuddsoddiadau yn y tywod
Eiddo ar fenthyg am y llog uchaf, hawliau
Diamod ar gynnyrch llafur o draethau aur y byd.

Nyni, etifeddion diwylliant gwâr yr oesoedd
Mwynhawn ddarnau amheuthun seigiau diymadferth
Y wledd ddiderfyn rhwng yr haul a'r gwin.'

Ebychiad

Geiriau
Eiddo pwy
Eiddo pawb
Cyfoeth gwerin gwlad
Yn cuddio
Mewn coedwig eiriadurol
Fel adar mân
Hadau cyfundrefn
Yn aros atgyfodi

Eu hela yw eu rhyddhau
Hyd galan gaeaf y byd

Geiriau
Cymryd arnom
Hawl heboga

Geiriau gwg
Geiriau gwamal gwag
Hylif ymadrodd trwynol
Yr iaith lywodraethol
Y modd gorchmynnol
Try wythiennau gwddf
Yn dyrau traha

Ninnau mewn salmau
Llam a naid
Penawdau
Etifeddwn
Haint ufuddhau

Sŵn llyfu llyffetheiriau
Llifeiriant mân siarad
Cyfathrebu brwd
Dadleuon ffug
Paderau parch
Cyflwynwyr agos atoch

Gwleidyddion rhesymegol
Rhesi o ddannedd gosod
Yn ymarfer o flaen y drych

Geiriau
Eiddo beirdd
Carffosiaeth is-ymwybod
Arian mân
Y meddwl byw

Geiriau
Etifeddiaeth babanod
Gwynfyd chwarae plant
Cystrawen hen freuddwydion
Unig hawlfraint penglog
Gair ar garreg fedd.

Raptus

Angel neu ysbryd
Preswylydd cyfrin pa ofod bynnag sy'n bod
Rhwng nef y nef a'r nenfwd
Angel anneall ysbryd anamlair
Tu mewn ac nid tu hwnt i'r llen

A'r gallu gennyt i drawsnewid
Lliw ffenestr gwyll a gwawr

Dyro i ni eto fflach o'r weledigaeth
Sy'n troi'r bydysawd fel modrwy ar fys bach

Dyheuwn amdanat, chwiliwn fel hen gariadon,
Ysglyfaeth soriant a siom
Yn anrheithio tir eu gorffennol
Am greiriau hoen, olion hen hapusrwydd,

A'th gael hwyrach fel cyw melyn cyntaf
Yn crynu rhwng bysedd ofnus plentyn
Ennyd perlesmeiriol cynnyrch eiliad
Cynhaliaeth oes.

Cara Signora

'Why do birds sing?' 'Why indeed.'
She sits on the kitchen chair blinking in the sun
Her wreathed hands withering in her lap.
At eighty-six she is reappraising
The nature of existence. 'The yellow bird
In the medlar tree never sings. Neither do I.
But I am still a living substance.'
'Surely,' we say. ' But of course.' Our function,
Foreign guests with baskets on their arms
Is to stand in the heat and absorb her steady moan.

'People know me. The *principe* shows me respect
He calls me *cara signora*. So why
Should that woman my only son has married
Want to kill me?'

    Her single eye
Is the pin that holds the landscape in position.
The edges of the view curl like a postcard
In the sun. The hens scratch under the olive trees.
Luigi the only son labours in the orchard.
Camilla the aforesaid daughter-in-law lurks
In her bedroom straining her ears as she applies
A new deodorant under her arms.

'She's a plundering murderess. That's what I call her.
She wants to kill me. Then she'll kill him.
Finish him off when I'm out of the way
If I had weapons sharper than words
I'd run her through, the witch, the whore . . .'

A judge in black delivers her shrivelled verdict.
Poor Camilla. There never was a woman less
Like a witch or a whore. An infants' teacher
As she was and her voice as sweetly virginal
As ever it was and her only vice
As she would be the first to confess
A weakness for chocolate.

'And to think I forced the spoon-fed lout
To marry her. Can you imagine it?
To gain an heir of course and make
A man out of a spoilt adopted child.
What did he do all day except take
Photographs of ruins or draw plans
Of empty churches. Fail his exams
And make excuses. That's the way he was
Pining to make a splash and yet
Too lazy to qualify and I, would you believe it,
Stupid enough to defend his curly head
From my husband's heavy hand.
And here's my reward. Sitting like a sick cat
In the sun moulting and struggling for breath
As useless as a cough. Decaying
In public. Do you hear me? Life
Is a conspiracy not a proverb.'

We stood still eager to move. Guests
On their way to drink sweet wine and cakes
At plump Camilla's table before
Going out to gather figs and tomatoes
In Luigi's three-acre orchard. Or was it hers?
Who owns what sings the surface of the lake
As it grins at the sun.

'That's the way he was my son until he married.
Work-shy. Skin like a girl. But now
He's sweating from morning till night
All muscle – a fully grown farmer
Besotted with a fat barren wife.

They're emptying my house you know and selling
My pieces and he is as indifferent
To me as a stone or a postage stamp.
So to whom should I turn? The *questura*?
The *carabinieri*? He slinks away and leaves
A space where a boy used to be. The *Sindaco*
I spoke to him in private and do you know
What that foul-mouthed communist said?

In his view the law should never meddle
In domestic polemics – and me well aware
The ugly brute and his stupid father before him
Used to beat his wife and children . . .
Emptying my house piece by piece
How much respect should the half alive show
To the half dead?'

Not a breath of wind. The *bandiera rossa*
Hangs like an empty political sleeve
From the Monaldeschi tower. And she expects
To be greeted by every passer by, especially
The 'Old Prince' as they call him on his way
To mass. High days and holidays he would kiss
Her hand and call her his *cara signora*.

'A plague on all daughters-in-law! This bitch
Has a mincing mother skulking in a sty
In a back street of Viterbo. Before I'm buried
She'll be parked in my feather bed
And she'll sit here I suppose in this very chair
And the 'Old Prince' on his way to mass
Will kiss her paw – his sight is bad –
And call her his *cara signora*.
Tell me, you have great learning and come
From another country. Is it the same wherever you go?'

She sits in front of her door a black idol,
A prisoner in paradise. How many picture
Postcards are needed to hide her pain?
For us there was no choice except
To practise a kiss on her withered cheek
Before passing indoors to greet her daughter-in-law
With appropriate effusion.

Show Business

The extra was shot in the doorway.
His face showed the final agony
But the director wasn't best pleased.
'Goddamit', he said. 'You faggot. Don't you know
How to die?'
He was over budget, behind schedule
And his wife had left him.

'Let's change the set-up,' the director said.
'The guy gets knifed from behind. That way
We won't get to see that sheep's face and those piss-hole eyes.'

It wasn't called for, the extra said to himself.
This is the only face I've got and this
If you bother to look is a golden day
The world's colours are singing. Quietly
The wind has curled up in his white cave. This is the season
When men and women and dogs can walk on water.
I'm not a vacant shape. My thoughts
Are worth sharing, my sympathies
Like the autumn light or the biosphere
Spread over all.

Lunch break the extra hankered to make contact:
So much so he would even apologise
For a fault that was never his. The director
Crushing aspirin to wash down with vodka and coke
Turned away. The extra offered him his doughnut.

'I need to be more savage,' he said.
'I can see that. If decapitations are called for
We can't object to the flies. After all
Death is nothing to be afraid of. Bodies
Are expendable. It's souls that count.'

'Don't nobble me now, brother,' the director said.
'This is Art not Nature. Can't you see
I'm wrestling with the fucking Gestalt.
Go talk to the view.'

'The view is relevant,' the extra said.
'I think that is the point I am making.
We need to squeeze our being into a wider context.
Like history books we provide a service.
Under your skilled direction your cameras capture
Machine-guns harvesting the rush hour streets,

But today is also the solstice when the sun
Becomes transparent and bird-song shrinks
To twigs like marginal notations printed
Black against a parchment sky,

The river of time flows backwards.
The king of the underworld and his attendants linger
Outside our skulls ready to accept
Arrears of rent. In the burial chambers
Like housing estates overlooking the luminous sea
The brides of silence are stirring in their dusty beds.
Set your microphones to catch their sighs and . . .'

'Look,' the director said. 'You pretentious creep.
Beat it. Piss off and don't come back.
You're fired.'

Motet

i

Read this and understand it
The message read. There are
Intermediaries less elusive than words
Languages that need not vanish, visitations
That never cross the threshold and never
Leave the hearth. Paint can dance
Laughter is the promise of a presence
That will bring peace with its unrest.

ii

Where the oystercatchers foregather
Under a grain of sand lies the secret.
Shuffling words like counters may help
Some people to think but that process
Is outside creation. In the cave by the sea
Shell shards seaweed are their own
Concordance. With the yellow sand
They propose the quantity of peace
Available between cosmic storms.
Here they store their title deeds before
And after the battle but not inside
Word boxes. The tide reads
The language of the water, feeds
Myths and messages along the shore,
Fingers a wet philology like a mother
Looking for a name.

iii

In the archbishop's palace
Cadenzas occurred when the instruments were silent
Flowed through particles of light with operatic names
Towards the alpine gardens and among the leaves
The birds of guilt and innocence shift like twin shadows
Doubt and certainty and there were glimpses
Of the arrow of time bending: in music
The notes dance like angels on the pinhead
Of a pause.

The world can speak. Merlin's stones
Can move of their own volition
Without his incantation
After the point of departure the continent
Drifts in the shape of a question:
We are fulfilled with ignorance
And as he said from where the flies
Curdle the air and the sun bakes
Foreign skins, to this sweet solitude
The self same sea is capable of opening
Mouths like green bells, soft green bells
That fall back in their effort
To devour themselves.

We have a function. Like alpine flowers
We snuggle our roots between the hard rock
Of perception. White and tender
We protect our lives developing
Prehensile power and as time
Keeps strict account learn to accept
The sea the rocks the air as personal gifts
Slowly sung on our skin.

Postcards

i

Does this picture please?
The tide fingers the same wavering line
Where you stood goddess of the salt spray
And the same seagull's beak
Draws silk threads of time between sand and sky
And calls for your return . . .
There's nothing wrong with hiraeth
If it lifts the heart
And charts the limit of a vast estate
Where the last wave humbly licked
Your children's trembling feet.

ii

What's the point of even saying 'hello'
Or muttering like a tide-race to yourself
If you have so little to say to this ex-commander
Except envy the ribbons on his chest, so little to say
To the rich widow and her dogs, the former centre-forward,
The newspaper man on his hols. I could offer
A drink in each case and sing out
'Iechyd da' but then what? Embrace
The waitress and apologize for the mistake?
Strange talk without a common tongue
But stranger still to share a language
And have nothing to say to each other.
O southern night fall like gratitude
On my shoulders, separate the days
And bless the return ticket
As it nestles between my armpit and my heart.

iii

Everywhere lovers are victims
Of their own desires. If they survive
They return to the landscape they themselves laid waste
The door is a one-eyed giant
The snail track of memory glistens on a broken wall
The air is too thin to breathe. The guardian

Stumbles in the courtyard. The flame
Flickers in his lantern. The search
Is penitential

As we trample among the ruins
Longing for relics. The visions we encounter
Are ghosts of children eating shreds of time

In the dry river bed
We snatch at fool's gold
And wait for stone to tremble
Between cold fingers like a day-old chick

Weak with fear but eager for release
On the floor of a new heaven.

iv

Remorseless package. Those dogs
Have throats like wolves. The wind from the sierra
Barks through the heat. Do I belong here?
The cords of my existence have been stretched
Too far leaving the dark laws of space
And shrivelling stars to hold together
The living and the dead, to nail the pines
The boats the tall hotels the swimming pools
In their several places: only your absence
Preserves the universe from imminent collapse.
Before my eyes the silent hosts of twilight
Disarm the living: about my feet
The dry leaves rustle like lost souls.

v

What is the point of flying
In a shrinking world? Hurling yourself
Like a codfish or a tadpole from pool to pool
Landing on foreign soil at midnight
And seeing yourself as un-nourished as a ghost
In the pitiless mirror of another airport bar.
There must be more to it
Suppose we impersonate some other species

170

Octopi, for instance, with more arms
To embrace our native rocks
Grow tentacles of blind affection
Prepare to hug one place
For at least a millennium
Prepare to wait
With the patience of the sea itself
For that visitation.

vi

Angel or spirit
Consoling presence
Secret inhabitant of whatever space
Rules between these ribs of stone
And heaven

Angel of unknown speech
Spirit that masters silence

Tear down this veil
Transform the stained glass windows
Of the dawn the dusk

Give us that sudden vision
That turns the universe
Like a ring on a little finger.

vii

How can my world end
Sang the enigmatic poet
While the cloud hovers overhead
And the virgin walks on the cloud
Like the presence that proves
Like the brilliant need
Like the young girl's face
That annunciates
The value of this world

This is the vine in the sun and this
The light that filters through the summer leaves

171

This is the element of play that turns
The void into a garden
Waiting into meaning
Loving as common as daylight

Age swallows memory
But not the expectancy
Or the readiness to listen
Let me hear again
Time beating in her wrist

And see her walk
And hear the nightingale
The voices of the children
Entitled to assemble
Where the light of her countenance
Illuminates our corner of the last garden.

Inscribing Stones

i

Ar ôl y glaw daeth arysgrif i'r golwg ar y traeth
I brofi bod adar hefyd yn medru sgwennu.
Gan ddieithred yr iaith, 'does gen i'r syniad lleia'
Be'n union oedd y neges.
'Ta waeth am hynny, chwedl ein doethuriaid cyfathrebol,
Gyda hyn daw hwrdd o wynt heibio
I ddarllen a dileu.

Ddydd a nos geilw'r elfennau a'r milod ar ei gilydd
Heb sylwi dim ar y deallusion
Fel cerrig nadd yn sefyllian o gwmpas y lle
Ac am wn i cystal diolch am hynny.

ii

Who am I who was she
Something or nothing
According to the magnitude of our illusions
She stepped out of a place and time
Like a goddess born in the water
And each drop that clung to her skin
Was a contamination

So it has always been
Our skins are toughened by contact
Not with other skins but with
The corrosive acid of contemporaneity
These are the vestments of pollution
That make us who or what we are
And puzzle our descendants.

Aurelius Augustinus, that saintly man,
In whose past so many enemies
Sniffed with unhealthy interest
Whispered as he shed his skin
The comforting formula and we repeat it:
Each age each epoch each period
And therefore each living second
Is equidistant from eternity

And in this only lies our hope.
My dear, our so called undying affection
Is also a mote in the beam
That twists around our planet
And burns a sun in its grip.

iii

Damia'r beirdd. 'Y cyfyngiad mwyaf
Dinistriol yw cenedligrwydd'
'Pen ni werthid er punnoedd', wir
'Pen glan fal Ieuan oedd . . .'
I'r bin â'r fath ofergoel
A'i gladdu mewn tomen o gymhorthdal

Hen wlad ei dadau
O na byddai mur dur o gwmpas dy bur hoff bau
A brawdoliaeth Wyddelig arfog
Ar ddiorffwys wyliadwriaeth dros
Raeadrau eisteddfodol a'r gorseddogion
Yn tywallt llifogydd o gynganeddion
Yn lle gwaed i lenwi'r ffosydd.

Ymladdwn oll ddydd a nos dros yr hawl
I gynnal nosweithiau llawen ar gamera
A syllu mewn syndod
Ar gwrs y byd yn troi'n bapur wal.

iv

Nid talwrn yw'r byd
Ac eto mae'r ffiniau'n cau amdanom

Embrace me ancient muse
But not too close
Clutch my tongue
With the language of my fathers

Cofleidia fi, awen y cynoesoedd

Words are more delicate than grass
You bend the stem

174

Grind seedheads
And what have you to invest
Except broken joints
And discoloured hands

Obligations are awesome
Llyffetheiriau tynn yw llyfrau'r meirwon

We can't live like swifts
In the summer heat harvesting
The trees above the thin river
For just another season
We are more inclined to make a stand
A self-conscious species collating
Strategies of survival, finding
Arms to overcome forgetfulness.
Consume us and conserve us
Language of our fathers
As we cross ourselves and cross
The desert to the unknown state
Where it all began.

v

Gan fod popeth o dan haul
Yn hysbysebadwy
Ond y gwir, neilltuwn
Ein hiaith leiafrifol
Ar gyfer y celwyddau golau mwyaf gwefreiddiol
Pan beidia'r bobl â gwrando
Bydd marw mwy na barddoniaeth.

vi

Yn orlawn o lwyddiant, wedi ei arwisgo
Â'r parch sy'n ddyledus i uchel ddiwylliant yr oesau
Ah yes gilded with respect
Easy for you to indite
Inside your laurel leaves
Concerning a universe due
Like a bubble not so much
To burst as to divest itself
Of its short-lived contents

Save us our syllable. We need
Our cloak of superstition if that's the word
To keep us warm: spider's webs
To heal our wounds

We suffer from a different desperation.
No rights of surfeit no rebellious rites
Against an indulgent god

We are up to our necks as they say
As long as the struggle lasts

And if the estate of the stars
Drifts in a cosmic bubble
Our little world is a water-bell
That trembles in space
Making its own nervous music

Ymdroi dros dro felly
Mewn swigen anfeidrol ei maint
Gan ymarfer o'r newydd
Holl wychder
Heintiau bod.

vii

Ar doriad gwawr yn methu cael ei wynt
Rhoes ei lythyrau caru i'm gofal
Fel bara cudd. Wn i ddim
Hyd y dwthwn hwn beth oedd ei fwriad
Yn cynnig imi ddyfroedd lladrad ac yntau
Druan yng nghysgod y dyfnder poeth:
Gosod arnaf chwedl, cyfrinachau anhydrin,
Cruglwyth o lwon melys nad ydynt
Bellach o bwys yn y byd i neb.

I knew them both. He hid his feelings
Like a lonely trapper in the forest burying
Provisions for a heth that never came
And she on the back benches sat ageing
Under peroxide as she waited smiling
For the call that also failed to arrive.

A plot that never thickened.
Fel hyn y mae pob hen gredo yn hel llwch.

viii

Who does history belong to, cries the adolescent
Wriggling above her homework. I can't bear it
And you can't tell me

Ask the Goth when he rides in, but don't forget
He strangled the historian.
Hitler stamped on Paris
But it barely shook
Jefferson dreamt as he drank
The river of progress of canals
Turning purple and
Navigational networks
Like wet sheep dogs bringing
A continent to heel

Idle reflections. Not so random. Every seventh
Or maybe seventieth year let the Tablets
Be reassessed and bones shifted
From the earliest tombs.

Whose history indeed but yours,
Emerging angel. Such dust as it rises
Will powder the transient bloom on your cheek

Cherish the Past where every door
Opens for a lifetime on the inside of your eyelid
Old women's eyes are magic. In that miracle
Untamed you will be fourteen again
Ready to eat the world and equally willing to be eaten.

ix

Camp addysg, fy mechan i, yw ymwrthod â
Phendantrwydd efengylaidd.
Nid oes, er enghraifft, angen profi
Mai dylyfu gên y lleuad
Yw trai a llanw hanes

Swydd athro, pennaeth doeth, yw cadw trefn
Ar rialtwch diymwared ffeithiau

177

Cadw cyfri hynny yw, cadw gwylnos
Cyn yr ecsodus a ddaw
Fel seindorf silicotig
I arwain y genedl o'r cymoedd

Gan besychu o garreg filltir
I garreg filltir
Cyn cyrraedd y maesdrefi
Yng ngolwg y môr

A sgleinio ei hepil fel lampau pres
Trosiadau bregus i groesawu
Arwyr yr oes newydd o Ealing, Disneyland,
A Slough.

x

Dâr a dyf
Rhwng llynnoedd y canrifoedd

The lane they say
Lies waiting.
Another spring arrives.

It leads need I add
To the lodestone church
And the graveyard where
The sensual seasons
Disport themselves like
Ghostly children
Among the headstones
And trample
(Hirymarhous eu darmerth)

The seeds that shed
Oblivion
Here where it was all
First thought of
Anonymity in ritual robes
Inscribing stones
Comes to rest.
History's harvest
Home.

S.L. i R.S. (An Imagined Greeting)

i

Let it be understood poets
Are dangerous: they undermine
The state: they thrust
Before congregations hymns
They would prefer not to hear.

Lyric terrorists disrupt
The best ordered families drive
Favourite sons abroad
In seach of nameless ecstasies:
Incite wives and daughters to dance
Before the flickering images
Of unattainable desires . . .
Who knows what supernovae
Are detonated in
A universe of sleeping hearts?

ii

You arrived at an unexpected
Hour, emerged
From that Austin Seven
Like an ostrich stretching
His legs as he abandons
The mechanised egg
Eyes washed in primal light
Unused to blinking.

Integrity is a lyric gift
Not a virtue: be warmed for a lifetime
By the hammering of
Unfettered thought
On the anvil of your suffering.

iii

Plato should have consulted
Gwydion Ddewin before
Sending your soul into exile.
Dâr a dyf rhwng dau lyn.
A poet can become a bird
So that intelligent pigs can feed
On the flesh as it drops
From the burning branches.

iv

Er gwaethaf neu oherwydd
Dy gathlau ysblennydd
Ieithwedd anorfod
Gorfoledd a chur
Yn dy galon y Gymraeg a orfu.
Dyna pam y saif cawr
Awenydd a'r oerwynt
Yn ymlid ei gydynnau gwyn
O flaen Llys Barn yn erfyn
Ar y cenedlaethau achub
Ei cham: aderyn y gwyll
Yn ymarfer cân y wawr.

Who's Speaking?

Ultimate discoveries
Are made in winter
Snow on the bridge
And galaxies piercing the sky
Pinpricks in the velvet
Choreograph small lives
With giant steps, expose
Eyes in exile with distances
That defy calibration:
How far is far when it
Embraces near?

But this is summer:
Sounds of the world
Are drifting in through open windows
As familiar as handwriting
With the same hint of truth
Aching to manifest itself
Through a notation of silence

Whatever came into existence
In that mythic winter
Persists; a spider's thread
Of experience suspended
Like a piece of debris in outer space
That intermittently catches the sun
And threatens the sky with
The glitter of inexplicable messages.

iii

The twilight for an old man
Is a procession of spectres
They come sidling in, shy
And familiar, tics and gestures
Smiles in the doorway of the mind
Hands raised and sweetly
Balanced between
Resurrection and dissolution

iv

Outside the narrow door
Lie darkness and the dark sisters
There are tunnels should you
Need to travel and a choice of guides
From one safe haven to another
Faces you never touch voices
That carry meaning
More penetrating than words

v

I called on one of your off-days
Whether you were in or not
I thought I caught your answer
Or was it an echo: 'Take hold of things.'
What was the radio source which star
Is capable of singing which sphere
Contains the vast wilderness
Where desires are transmuted into storms.
So many reservations
In the corridors of a faithless heart
How can the song of the red dwarf
Ring true in the river of time?

vi

You own a piece of my soul
A vulgar fraction. What is left
Is a phantom articulating love
In borrowed words like
Molecules resembling
Forgotten runes while
Another season eludes our grasp.

The whiff of eternity persists
Like the glow of childhood, not just
Here and there but everywhere
And forever like standing stones
Mud under foot, the fading colour
Of weeds along the hedegerow
So that the sparrow's trembling wing
Transmits the old message:
Immortality lurks in the deep space
Between memory and oblivion.

Counting the Dead, Winter 1942

Jubilate Deo in a dark unheated church
And outside victims howling for protection
The whole earth closes its eyes. Landscapes
Sculpted by a giant sigh shrink
Into our sarcophagus

The German boots that trudged two thousand
Miles to Stalingrad the milk white horse
Startled to death by a shadow in the trees
All drawn into the abyss of hope

Counting on frozen fingers the hated self
At last has merged into the only world
That can accept it

The abiding stench of racial war
Genocide drifting which ever way
The wind that was designed to save us
Turns

Life is treachery. Only Death
Is loyal. The god we worship
Has declared living irrelevant
Only uniforms are bearable
To breathe in blue with cold
The only bodies to embrace
To be alive is a disgrace.

Hitler's Teeth

Chill in the hand
They cannot bite
History they say
Was never like this
When that hot mouth
Bawled out
The triumph of the will

They say
These bit off more
Than they could chew
His sibilants
Withered
City walls

Sewers exploded
Rats marched, teeth
Flashed in the sun
Carpets burned
In the spittle

But not enough
They say
The bridge work
Could not match
A vegetarian appetite
For slaughter

Unable to revert
To milk teeth
They gnaw
Their sterile cage
Scaled and polished
With damnation.

That Summer

There was nothing to help us
Trapped in that ornamental summer
By sunlight and ubiquitous foreboding: the tides
The pebbles indifferent to our sore feet
Told us nothing: banner headlines
Congealed those lukewarm fish and chips.

From where we stood to the horizon
The future stretched like a brooding canvas
Awaiting a blood-stained brush. There were rocks
And groundsheets to sleep on, nowhere to go.
Only the tanks knew where to assemble.

Who would win who would lose
Whose corpse would hang on the wire
Would come later. The seagulls knew
More than we did as they wheeled above us
Like fighter bombers, their droppings
Illegible leaflets, mobilising their screeches
As they crossed and recrossed concrete
Frontiers reinforced in the Underworld.

It didn't need to happen. It shouldn't
But it would. Limbs still free
Twitched with the urge to run: the sea
Was a threat not a refuge: the sky
Was closing in. We could only turn and face
The mouth of the tunnel: only wait
For the machine to emerge and howl
On our behalf as it ran us down.

The Life Peer

Anything with the word 'Welsh' in it
Upsets me. Don't ask me why.
Possibly it was my mother's fault
Or more likely my father's. They both behaved
As if they had something to hide
And so what was it? Not just a language

What do words themselves matter. *Tlawd*
A *balch* is only poor but proud. Means nothing.
It went deeper. Conquered of course
Beaten down. Disgraced. What else? Somewhere
Somewhere in the smouldering past someone
Escaped. Ran away. Deserted the ritual slaughter
Where he should have lain cold and graceful
Embracing honourable oblivion. He snared
Shall we say a swineherd's idiot daughter
And made her pregnant: bloodshed
And furtive rapine saved a race. Greed
Accumulated a so-called Heritage.
Is that all it amounts to?

My prospects of office are bleak. I shall
Resign and spend my well-earned rest
In a more accommodating climate. English
Speaking of course. Key Biscayne calls.
My wife assures me all the courts
Are stately and uniform. Our heads shall
Turn in unison and watch the world's best bodies
Cavort on artificial grass as expensive
And unruffled as ermine.

A Public Meeting

The tenets of freedom are
Something to sing about
In any language
Like the weather they need
Extra terrestrial sunbursts
To be sustainable

The only progress that matters
He maintains is the progress of the soul
Which come to think of it
Must be wide enough for the welfare
Of all the others

For this reason Madam chairman
Our society needs a holy man
Not necessarily in a cave
Or in a prison but on the pavement
Living on very little and
Demonstrating
Against all the evidence
An unstinting love of passers by.

Oscar

Wordless we sit in the green shade
Outside the Cafe Lorenzo
Where the oranges hang like lamps
Of promise on Caterina's trees.

Nothing more difficult than to think
Of nothing: to transpose
From aging frames the weight
Of consciousness requires,
You say demands, more
Than the dance of particles

We are due, if not overdue
To embark on the weightless
State as heavy as gravity

But your hands are not as old
As mine as they leave the glass
To touch a fallen flower

The petals lie like
The true ghosts of being
And yet you say the colours
Of this world are not transferable

Only aspirations
Like *cançons populars*
Stretch up our necks
To contemplate the galaxies

The sparks fly upward
All we leave behind
You say is baggage
And the remorseless weight
Of unforgiving Time.

Andrée

Earthbound, the stage
Is nailed to the floor,
Down those glittering stairs
She comes in search of heaven
Spotlit
With a female swagger
Artificial starlight in her eyes

This gives us something of her
But nothing of her shyness
She lives inside illusion
Fragile but held together

As firmly as any earth mother
With vernal expectation

Not to take or measure
But to give
With more largesse
Than Balearic sunlight

Moreover
The shores of other islands
Warm as legends
Where a strut becomes a stroll
Lie in wait
For the white magic of Olwen's feet.

Tomos Tŷ Calch

A plug of tobacco hides inside that rosy cheek
Like a worm inside an August apple
He counts potato rows in Cymric twenties
And spits brown darts to fall
As arbitrary as flying bombs
Into an ordered ocean of green leaves.

This is summer in wartime
And his white moustache can stretch from ear to ear.
He says his *mingefn* hurts: and still
Shaped like his clothes by the long
Procession of eroding seasons
He sweats and smiles.

If he should reappear today at ebbtide
Stumping along the foreshore spitting and chewing,
The day's work ended, scraping
Those loyal hob-nailed boots outside his cottage door,
I shall ask him what he really thought
Of a pallid youth with girlish hands
Coughing under a cascade of sheaves and thistles.

I shall wait inside and kneel on stone
Until his leathery thumb sinks on the latch
And in he walks a servant transformed
By signs and seasons into an old master
Entitled to call a whole lost world
His own.

Cae Llanol

Interred in obsolete language
They shed his patronymic. *Pater
Vester qui in caelis est.*
The silence sings

And it is enough. Unquenchable
Faith spelt out his name
With a sickle G and a hybrid
R memorialised from a lost book
Uncial incisions
Stratify a sparse message

Rejoice. I shall rise again
My consciousness was more
Than a brittle sigh breathing
Only the present tense

Hic iacet buried faces
And a glowing future
Outside the dissolving cities
Nothing to gainsay
The secret music of
An island sky

Be reassured.
In this field
Love moved like a lantern in the dark
His shadow built
The fragile ladder that led
Through a shallow grave
To his depth of heaven.

The Pest Controller

He came to dispose of them, dressed for the part.
'Wasps', whistling and humming, 'like
The human race,' laughing, 'are a pest
And I'm taking no chances. Work
Is work of course. We all need to earn
Our crust but my true delight –
And I don't mind telling you – is singing.'

He was humming away as he set the wheels in motion.
'Can't have a wasps' nest within inches
Of your sleeping head. No way. I'm a second tenor
So what's wrong with playing second fiddle?
Nothing if you're the treasurer of the male voice choir.

Wasps have vicious tempers but as far as I know
They don't sting each other. Now I've got
A cassette in the van. Would you like to hear it?
No not me. It's forty years old for God's sake
And that voice is as clear as a bell
More than a bell. It lifts me you know
As I go from job to job. Keeps me going.

It's a hymn he's singing, prayer
Urgent prayer flows through his skull
And a benediction takes him by the throat.
There was whisky there too mind you
His favourite tipple. My old Uncle Jack,
My grandmother's brother, was with him
In the Welsh Guards. They used to go
Drinking and singing hymns together.
Happy days. War or no war. Mind you
They say it ruined his career

But the hymns still work. The time you get
Bitten is when you take the plastic armour
Off. I got bitten once in the mouth.
Couldn't sing for a month. Here we go. Smoke
And bellows. Wasps have their music. What's it to be,
Lads? Martyrs of the Arena or Crossing the Plain?'

The Day I Forgot your Name

I don't claim you were central
To my existence: but without
A periphery there can be no centre.

Not even an initial. That was bad.
And the signal stinging the nerve ends
Many are called but few are chosen
And since you rarely chose me, your name
But not your presence has tumbled
Over the cliff of memory and all that remains
A frayed and brittle rope twitching
Between disordered fingers.

Everybody counts of course they do
Dead or alive they need a number
And there needs to be a galactic mass
From which a mote in heaven's eye
Can emerge and resonate beyond
The nagging fragment of a tune.

Half my adult life to the point
Of furtive imitation I admired you
Your antiseptic smile and measured pauses
Coolness personified

So how can I retrieve my balance
Without digging up this library
To uncover at least the first letter
Of your name.

Contradiction

Rhyl could be anywhere he said. I assured him
It wasn't so to me and could never be
Anything less than a fulgent mirage filled
With chapels and pleasure domes in unequal parts
And a promenade like a prairie shaved for Forthcoming Attractions.
Here God and Mammon doze in deck-chairs
While their offspring search the sand-dunes
For laws and prohibitions they can safely break.

There is more to the place than any heroin
Addict or colour-supp photographer
Could ever guess. Clocks tick backwards
Cinemas burn incense with scented celluloid
And in every chemist shop they give away
Prayer books as well as condoms.

Streets are paved with toffee. Seagulls
Nest in towers built of eccles cakes.
Toilets and old-time dancers line up
In psychedelic colours that were all
The rage before the world grew up. Ghosts
On tricycles dodge between councillors
As they polish their chains with perennial
Hope of a royal visit or at least a gala opening.

Be sage be savage be gentle. Mention Peacocks
And nothing over sixpence. Just pretend
For an eye-blink, times have never changed.

Bathroom Interrogation

Name? Timor.
Preferred state? Mildly excited.
Language? Mild also with
Fringes of surprise.

      [Mind you, some words stink
      With history, wrenched out of
      Other people's tongues, exhumed
      Still smelling they lurk
      Inside sentences tense

      Immigrants anxious to be employed
      And have their past ignored. Cleansed
      Smirking at face value
      Eager for display
      Savage *sluagh-ghairm*
      Spruced up into slogan . . .]

Enough of that. Age?
Second childhood not easily
Disentangled from the first.

Preferred season? Waiting
Life as expectation
Supple with the sap
Of recollection.

Favourite star? The furthest
That takes the longest
Look and still winks
With what I take to be approval
Of when it all began.

Listening to Messiaen

These are new devotions. The world to come
Glides and rustles among the trumpets
And the drums. The means and the measure. How else
Could you eavesdrop on the chatter of ghosts? Stringed
Promises can simplify our torments even
Overwhelm the percussive threat of retribution.

Orchestral instruments are physical machines
Sounds and sighs with souls inside them. Arguments
To celebrate the insistent heartbeat
Of the new born child: the miracle
In the manger on a starlit night:
The deliverance, the eternal arms.

Each man needs his secret and his craft
To thread the message armed with the grace notes
Of reconciliation, and at the least restore
Tenderness between the living and the dead.

Out of the walled garden and the intermediate state
Paradise creates a musical condition:
With mounting courage at the water's edge
It transports trembling souls across
That bridge of gossamer above the black abyss.

Contemplating a Yew Tree (Llanddeiniolen)

This is solid stuff. Planted deep
In its own damp history. Small
Scope for unattached imagination
This tree has its own dark vision

And he saw it stretch its
Well fed arms to cover
All the tombs that shrink
Inside its shadow

The one and only place. Pinned
As the earth turns
To this stony ridge
Locked in gates
More rigorous than iron.

He lies among them
Arm for arm and as he wrote
These still extend their own style
Of twisted syntax to restrain
Laughter and sunlight

Nothing to disturb the quiet
Of dead peasants that were
His own people one and all
To marvel at and to account
For his own disjointed presence.

As they fed him, now he and they
Feed the solemn tree: as all along
He knew it. The essential information
Is in our bones. Nostalgia
Was his fuel as it is now
Mine. We need he wrote
As he sulked in the tea room
Of the Mother of Parliaments to belong

And I don't belong here.
Moodier as his sister said
Than any woman in contempt
Of a national itch to be famous
And approved of, he analysed

His patient doting father,
All his devotions, treasurer
Of his chapel worshipping
In proper order God and Education
And the Empire that protected
Missionaries on his behalf.

History and hard reality
Crumble around the tree. He
Hardly hoped the dead would awaken
At the angry eloquence of
A would be whipping boy. He
Only knew they would assemble
Here to receive him

Just as the parish couples all those
Years ago came here to court
And dance those first steps
Of their pilgrimage fearless as
Insects in the green precincts
Of the King of Fear.

Single Mother

I am you and you are me
So far you've no idea
How that came to be
So I poke your cheek
And murmur baby mine

And you, don't hang your head
Don't dribble. You're alive
And well though your rotten
Father's fled.

Gone so early and so soon
Don't inherit
His weak eyes and hanging head
Laugh a bit
And scream sometimes.

He was negatively good.
There's a concept
Rarely understood
Don't you be the same
Other kids will come
Pinch and steal
If you don't look out
You'll always get the blame

You're better off
To be like me.
Don't dribble
Just take my nipple
Your lips are mine
My breast is yours.

Wrong Number

At sunset his thoughts
Were solid with numbers
His arteries hardening
Leather bound
With lavished sums

It was peace of a kind
The gold light poured through
The safety of the double glazing
Until the telephone bell
Pierced his defences

His hand trembled
With the prospect of being needed
Even by the scrounging wheedle
Of importunate heirs

He was mean they said
Nesting among his monies
Like a swallow in mud

Raising the receiver
A strange urge to share rose
Like the smell of stew
From a distant kitchen

A cry could be born
In the cradle a boon
A baptism spelt out
In rusty spittle

Alas as they say in legends
All he heard was a purring tone
In the sunlight a boon stillborn
And himself alone.

Marvao

He sprawls on the ramparts, burnt skin
Slack in the yellow sunlight. 'I like these walls.
No more bloodstains. Ideal for exiles
To lie on or die in. Ruins
To crawl about up and down. I'm as comfortable
As a cockroach.

As for you, don't be so restless. Nothing
Matters all that much. Except the booze
And the sun. And my dividends
Of course. They'll see me out. Tell them
I've gone native more or less
Without the lingo.'

Far below the swineherd and his pigs
Lurk in the cork forest. The shepherd
With his muted flock advances
             Through the olives to a conference
Not an encounter. They meet, weary generals
With their troops behind them held
In a Circean spell, chewing herbs.

'Come night,' sang the exile. 'Conjure up
Nirvana in an alien setting.
The rising mist will weave me
The blue cloak of comfort
And perpetual ease.'

Residential Home

Dozing in the afternoon you can confirm
Your mute palms as they touch become
Points of entry to a more soothing existence

Optimism is no longer indecent
The shrivelled skin you live in
Is not a cage buried in anaesthetic sand

You have a companion. Alcestis
In ripe old age ready to share the cost
Of the celestial journey that makes
No distinction between departure and arrival.

It is not in her nature to lament
Or pine while the emblem of a smile
Friendlier than the softest brush
Can sweep aside a dusty past.

Old age is pedestrian. Her footfall
Fading is more valid than a passport
And should lead you with assurance
Along the path to a place of light
Conjured out of the dark by the Ancient of Days.

Index of poem titles

Index of first lines